Helene von Damm has worked closely with Ronald Reagan since 1966. Given free access to his personal correspondence, she has chosen from his letters to GIs, students, political opponents, mothers, and Americans from every walk of life, and has woven them together into a fascinating narrative portrait of the politics and personality of one of today's most controversial, most admired, and most staunchly patriotic Americans.

Here are the private thoughts, the innermost sentiments, the deepest beliefs of the man himself.

Sincerely,

RONALD REAGAN

D1413929

SINCERELY,

Ronald Reagan

EDITED BY HELENE VON DAMM

BERKLEY BOOKS, NEW YORK

SINCERELY, RONALD REAGAN

A Berkley Book / published by arrangement with
Green Hill Publishers, Inc.

PRINTING HISTORY
Green Hill edition published 1976.
Berkley edition / July 1980

All rights reserved
Copyright © 1976, 1980 by Helene von Damm.
This book may not be reproduced in whole or in part,
by mimeograph or any other means, without permission.
For information address: Berkley Publishing Corporation,
200 Madison Avenue, New York, New York 10016.

ISBN: 0-425-04743-1

A BERKLEY BOOK ® TM 757,375
PRINTED IN THE UNITED STATES OF AMERICA

SINCERELY,
RONALD REAGAN

Contents

Foreword

RONALD REAGAN IS one of the great national leaders of our time, perhaps of any time. As I write this, his record of achievement on behalf of both his state and his nation rivals that of all but a few.

Too often men who attain such high position are viewed as expedient and ruthless leaders who have risen to power at the expense of or over the bodies of their peers. Too often men who rise to power, for all their initial good intent, become those kinds of people.

Ronald Reagan is almost unique in that after six years as president of the Screen Actors Guild, eight years as governor of California, and one major run for the presidency, he remains an honest, sensitive, caring human being with an unwavering faith in God and the essential goodness of man.

This book of his letters, updated to include the years between 1975 and 1979, is an accurate reflection of Ronald Reagan as I have come to know him, first as a fellow governor, then as chairman of his 1966 campaign for president, and finally, but always, as a friend.

His sincerity, his integrity, his beliefs, shine through in his own words as no biography or series of articles could make them do.

This is Ronald Reagan unrehearsed and unretouched. It is the real Ronald Reagan. As you read these letters and excerpts it becomes easy to see why he has risen from humble beginnings to touch the hearts and claim the loyalties of millions and why he may yet be elected president of these United States.

SENATOR PAUL LAXALT

Introduction

I LITTLE THOUGHT when I arrived in America from Austria that less than ten years later I would be personal secretary to the governor of our nation's most populous state.

"How did you ever get that job?" was probably the question most often asked by friends and strangers alike.

Well, it's a long story. I grew up during the war—and subsequently during the Russian occupation—in a small town in Austria where I lived with my parents and brother until I graduated from a nearby business college. After graduation, I moved to the big city, Vienna, where I got my first job as a secretary in a manufacturing company.

Adventuresome and ambitious by nature, I was determined to see more of the world before settling down and to achieve more than I thought was possible in a socialistic environment, so after two years, I moved on. I spent a summer in Sweden and a year in Germany until the opportunity to immigrate to the United States came along. As it was to so many before me, it was the realization of a dream—a promise of freedom and the opportunity to go as far as my ability and drive would take me.

For the first few years I lived in Detroit, working my way up from typist to an underwriter for a national insurance company. Probably because I had lived under both socialist and communist regimes, I early developed a keen interest in the political and governmental affairs of my new home. So I jumped at the chance to work for the political action committee of the American Medical Association—AMPAC. There I assisted the associate director in the preparation and staffing of conventions, supervised membership reports, and conducted research projects. I conscientiously followed the promises and actions of politicians and elected officials. When Ronald Reagan's message as candidate for governor of California reached me, it changed my life. I moved west to San Francisco to work in his campaign.

From then on, luck was on my side. After the election, one of the governor's appointees, Cabinet Secretary Bill Clark, asked me to go to Sacramento with him. This opened up a whole new world for me.

Along with other interesting duties, I had the fascinating job of recording minutes at the weekly cabinet meetings where all major administration decisions were being made. When after just a year my boss became the governor's chief of staff, I moved along with him, supervising and coordinating the activities in the executive unit. I enjoyed extensive personal communication with the cabinet, department heads, and members of the legislature. It was the kind of high pressure, often crisis-ridden atmosphere on which I thrive.

Then the governor's personal secretary resigned, and I was awarded that plum. For more than six years I managed his private office and staff, handled his personal correspondence, and coordinated his daily office schedule. This included the preparation of fully researched briefing memos for all office meetings.

I loved the diversity of tasks that went with my position: acting as Governor Reagan's representative with visiting dignitaries, heading the speakers bureau, and having the opportunity to accept dozens of speaking engagements from civic and Republican clubs throughout the state.

Most of all, I treasured my direct and frequent access to Ronald Reagan, governor of California.

At the conclusion of eight of the most exciting and rewarding years of my life, I searched for a way to pay tribute to the man who still commanded my highest admiration. I also wanted to share with others those experiences which helped me to maintain my idealism and my confidence in our system and future which so many Americans these days seem to lack.

I found no better way to accomplish my goal than to put

together a book of Governor Reagan's correspondence: letters not only to prominent persons but also to many fine men, women, and children of whom few have ever heard, but who are the kinds of people who make this country what it is.

I am deeply grateful to the governor for letting me go through and select the letters from him, and in some cases to him, that I thought reveal better than anything else possibly could the real Ronald Reagan—the man, his beliefs, his principles, and his character. The result was the first edition of this book, *Sincerely, Ronald Reagan.*

All this took place nearly four years ago. Since then, I have assisted Governor Reagan in his transition from public servant to private citizen, and in his new activities as columnist, radio commentator, and public speaker. As it was in the governor's office, these, too, have been hectic years, arranging public appearances and coordinating press, political, and business events throughout the country.

During his 1976 presidential campaign, I traveled and campaigned extensively in key primary states, speaking before local political and civic groups to promote this book of Ronald Reagan's letters.

Continuing public interest in Ronald Reagan has prompted me to update the book and to add three chapters to record through his letters the fascinating events of these years.

HELENE VON DAMM

A Long Way from Home

THERE ARE A few fortunate people who have been privileged to work closely with Ronald Reagan over a period of time. I am one of those lucky ones. With this background it is my pleasure indeed to write a book about this unusual man.

But whatever I might say about him would be colored by my own deep admiration of him, and, therefore, the truths about him that I would write would be suspect.

But Ronald Reagan's character, his warmth, his wisdom, and his philosophy of life all shine through the letters he writes to friends, to relatives, to other national leaders, and to strangers who have corresponded with him.

He is a man who feels obligated to answer personally the appeals, requests, and compliments as well as the criticisms and differences of opinion.

With his permission I have singled out some of those letters—letters that I believe help reveal the real Ronald Reagan.

The picture most people have of Ronald Reagan is of a tall, ruggedly handsome man, almost dapper in dress, urbane, witty, warm, yet somehow aloof. They remember him from his movies—there were fifty of them—from his television days, his spectacular speech for Barry Goldwater in 1964, his own campaigning, and his years as governor of California. Old-timers may recall him as Dutch Reagan from his sports-announcing days for radio station WHO in Des Moines, Iowa.

There is a glamor in all of this—radio, movies, television, and high-level politics. But there is little in any of it that recalls the poor boy from small-town Illinois, the summertime lifeguard who over a seven-year span rescued seventy-eight persons from drowning, or the rugged running guard at tiny Eureka College in rural Illinois.

But Ronald Reagan's background and the environment in which he grew up come through again and again to those who have worked with him. These roots have had a strong and lasting effect on Reagan the man and Reagan the husband and father, as well as Reagan the politician, the governor, the statesman, and the zealous defender of the American dream.

Ronald Wilson Reagan was born in Tampico, Illinois, but grew up largely in nearby Dixon on the Rock River. His father was John Edward Reagan, a first-generation black Irishman who sold shoes for a living—often not very successfully and sometimes not too soberly. This latter weakness left its mark on his younger son, Ronald, who, though no teetotaller, has seldom been known to have more than two drinks in an evening. His mother was Nelle Wilson Reagan, who instilled in Ronald the love for drama that eventually led him to Hollywood.

Ronald (early nicknamed "Dutch" by his father) and his brother Neil, who is two years older, grew up living the semi-idyllic Tom Sawyerish life of the typical small-town boy before the strident advent of radio, television, and the freeway.

In his autobiography, *Where's the Rest of Me*, written in 1965, Reagan describes this life. But underneath his gentle reminiscences one can discern how deeply his life has been affected by his childhood.

His father, a sentimental Democrat who believed fervently in the rights of the working man, also believed that every man should stand on his own feet. He had no use for bigotry in any form and refused to let his family see *Birth of a Nation* because it dealt favorably with the Ku Klux

Klan. He also once refused to stay in a hotel that did not admit Jews.

From his mother, who did dramatic readings as a hobby, Ronald inherited a love for drama which led him to participate in high school and college drama clubs, and eventually took him to Hollywood. From her, also, he received the fundamentalist Christian beliefs that even today strongly mark his letters, his conversations, his speeches, and his actions.

After high school the young Ronald Reagan worked his way through Eureka College where he played football, captained the swimming team, participated in campus dramatics, and worked on the yearbook.

Graduating in the deep depression days, he decided he wanted to become a radio sports announcer. In 1932 jobs did not come easily, but young Reagan hitchhiked from town to town seeking any kind of job in a radio station. After several months he found one, surprisingly as a sports announcer, on a station in Davenport, Iowa. The career that was to take him all the way to the governorship of California—and perhaps farther—had begun.

Memories of childhood and youth stay with us all. But Ronald Reagan's memories have been sharpened by requests from many persons to recall bits and incidents from his younger days. For instance there was the time a letter arrived at the Reagan home asking him to relate "the best advice I ever got." The advice came shortly after he was graduated from Eureka. It started him on his career.

"For seven years," Ronald Reagan recalls, "my last three in high school and my college years, I worked my way each summer as a lifeguard at a beach on the Rock River in my home town in Dixon, Illinois. It was located out in a kind of natural forest park. There was a rustic lodge, and a small group of families came there every summer. Many of them were second generation in summering at the lodge. I taught their children to swim. Most of the men were pretty successful, and many of them would speak to me about looking them up when I got out of college. They were sure they could find something for me.

"Then came the crash of '29 and the Great Depression. I graduated from college in '32 and returned for one last summer of lifeguarding. The men who said they would like to do something for me, now, had very real problems of their own. Anyone who did not live through the Great Depression can't have any understanding of what it was really like.

"One man, however, did say that if I could tell him what I wanted to do, and if it was in any one of several lines of work, he was sure that he had enough due bills out that he could get employment for me. At that time, of course, just a job, any kind of job, was almost a miracle. This man, however, insisted that I would have to tell him what line of work I wanted to get in, what particular field I felt I could have a future in. He said that was the answer he must have before he would go forward.

"Well, unlike so many of today's young people, and yet not unusual for that time, I had graduated from college still with no set idea in my mind of what course I should follow. In addition to athletics, my other great interest had been dramatics, and yet, living in the heart of Illinois—in those days never having been east of Chicago or west of the Mississippi River—one didn't go about saying, 'I would like to be an actor.' Radio was relatively new. Having played football, as well as other sports in high school and college, I finally mustered up the courage, under his prodding, to tell him that I would like to be a radio sports announcer.

"The field was relatively new, almost unexplored. I thought at least it was into the field of entertainment. Well, of course, I had named an occupation in which he had no connections and could do nothing for me. So then, he gave me that best advice. He said, 'Look, this is probably better. I could have gotten you a job (and he named several lines), but those who gave you the job would have been doing *me* a favor, not you; and, therefore, they would have considered they had done their part by simply giving you work. Now,' he said, 'you've mentioned a field that is new, that has a future. You must go out and start knocking on doors. You may have to knock on a couple of hundred of them—any salesman does before he makes a sale. You simply go in and tell them that you will take any job, including sweeping out, in order to get inside the industry and you will take your chances on working up from there; all you ask is a chance to work at anything within the industry.' He continued, 'Some place along the line, you'll find a man, who, even in spite of this depression, realizes that the world is going on and that he must be investing in new people, young people, if he is to have a future in the industry.'

"He was absolutely right. I started out hitchhiking, with only a few dollars in my pocket, trying station after station, usually failing to mention that I wanted to be a sports announcer—just simply saying that I would like to get into the announcing end of the trade—I figured sports announcing was a higher ambition that would come later—but telling that I would do anything, take any job, to get started.

"Sure enough, after knocking on a lot of doors, I came into a station, spoke to an unforgettable man who was the program director, a man who had come to this country from Scotland. This time, I mentioned sports, but otherwise my pitch was the same as it had been in all the others.

"This man gave me probably the most unusual audition that has ever been given. He put me in the studio all by myself, told me he'd be in another room where I couldn't see him, listening, and when the red light came on, I was to imagine a football game, broadcast it, and try to make him see it. Well, that is what I did—for about fifteen minutes. He walked back into the studio and told me to be there on the following Saturday—I was broadcasting a Big Ten game, the Iowa-Minnesota homecoming game.

"And that was the start of everything that has happened since. But the advice that led to that was the thing—that it isn't necessary to have pull, or to have someone get you a position. If you really have the faith, and will decide what it is you want to do, and then go out and knock on enough doors, you will find someone willing to gamble on even the most inexperienced person, as I was."

From his earliest days Ronald Reagan has struggled with the correct pronunciation of his name, as did his father before him. Although his family has always pronounced the name as if it were spelled "Raygan," Americans typically pronounce it "Reegan." Many people who have pronounced it "Reegan" feel that the governor himself changed the pronunciation to "Raygan" as an affectation and they look upon what they think is a change as being not quite honest. Even after his eight years as governor that feeling persists among some Californians, a number of whom have written him, accusing him not only of changing the pronunciation but also of such sins as dyeing his hair.

Here is an excerpt from a typical response by Governor "Raygan."

"My entire life and that of my family has been spent in a struggle to convince people that our name was pronounced Ragan. I was eight years old when I remember my father as we were moving to a new town, protesting that now he would have to start teaching another group of neighbors how to pronounce our name. Always everyone has tried to call it Reegan. Even though I had the opportunity on the air to sign off and pronounce my own name correctly, others insisted on the mispronunciation.

"You said you had an innate suspicion of someone who would change his name or dye his hair. I think if the opportunity would present itself, and you could have a close look, you would find not only is my name Reagan, but my hair is not dyed, and there is a salting of grey down the part to prove it."

Though people in public life often suppose the public knows all about them, the truth is that the public absorbs much misinformation from newspapers and other sources. On occasion the governor was constrained to set the record straight. The following is a letter to the editor of the *San Francisco Chronicle*, written in 1972 in response to a letter written about him by one Charles Goringe.

"Dear Sir:

"In the interest of perhaps saving you some future space in the letters-to-the-editors column may I (hopefully) set the record straight regarding my military service in World War II.

"For some time now I have watched the exchange of letters in your paper and been grateful to those who kindly wrote in my behalf. The others seemed to nurse a suspicion that my uniform was wardrobe from 'Western Costume Company' or that I laid claim to the Medal of Honor.

"The most recent letter from Charles Goringe of Redding had me commissioned a captain direct from civilian life serving under Col. Sam Greenwald (deceased), a Paramount news cameraman. Sam was a long-time friend and commanded a combat camera crew flying bombing and reconnaissance missions.

"One thing the letters have proven is that my book, *Where's the Rest of Me*, was not a best seller. That's strange too because it is the best book I've ever written—it is also the only book I've ever written. In it I devoted quite a few pages to my four years in the military and voluntarily made it clear that I never heard a shot fired in anger.

"Since you don't have a space for a synopsis let me briefly summarize. Prior to World War II, I was in the Army Reserve as a 2nd Lt. of Cavalry (horse cavalry that is, although I missed the battle of the Little Big Horn). I earned the commission in the usual manner, cheating only on the physical—my near-sightedness was below the acceptable standard. Prior to Pearl Harbor a routine physical without the help, this time, of a friendly examiner, reduced me to 'limited service' status. Following Pearl Harbor I was called to active duty and assigned to Ft. Mason. Later in the rapid expansion of the Air Corps I was transferred (not at my request) to the newly established unit of the Air Corps to set up to train combat camera crews, make training films, and photograph highly secret projects, which, as far as I know, may still be classified.

"This unit, 'The 1st Motion Picture Unit A.A.F.,' took over Hal Roach studios, a nearby academy, and an airfield. Most of our personnel was recruited and commissioned from the ranks of the studios and more than 75 percent were over age and physically ineligible for the draft. Frankly they did a good job and some of them must have been the highest priced K.P.'s in Army history.

"I ended my service when the war was over as a captain. The only effort I made in four years to influence my status in the service was a refusal to accept promotion to major.

"There were fourteen million Americans in uniform who didn't get overseas. I never knew one who wasn't conscious of the great inequity in the fortunes of war, aware completely and humbly of the debt we owe to those who did."

Mr. Goringe's letter as well as the governor's reply brought to the governor still another letter, this one from Sam Greenwald who protested that he was not yet dead.

Eureka College is a landmark in Ronald Reagan's life. When he attended in the late 1920s and early 1930s it had fewer than 300 students. Reagan got through by working part-time, working summers, and borrowing money, which he began repaying almost immediately upon graduation. He has been a member of Eureka's Board of Trustees, has donated generously to it through the years, has been awarded an honorary doctorate by it, and has participated almost as actively as an alumnus as he did when a student.

Here is an exchange of correspondence with Kip Hayden, editor of the *Pegasus,* the Eureka newspaper, who in 1974 sought a "Back in My Day" essay from the school's most famous graduate. In responding, the governor made it clear that he regrets not at all having attended a small school:

"In my job these past eight years I've been a part of big-time education as a regent of the University of California—all nine campuses and more than 100,000 students. All I've seen since has convinced me if I had it to do over again, I'd still go to Eureka. Just being elbowed in a crowd as 27,000 students go milling between classes isn't necessarily where the action is.

"One thing about Eureka, you can't remain anonymous. Students in the big assembly-line diploma mills can spend four years admittedly getting a good education, but never stretching themselves outside of their chosen studies to discover if they could participate in a play, sing in the glee club, make a team, or serve in a campus elective office. In a small college everyone is needed and there is no place to hide. If you make it in Eureka it's because your fellow students know you—not because they don't. And if you can make it under those circumstances you can make it anywhere.

"You are having a unique experience that is getting

harder and harder to find in academia. If we aren't very, very careful it may one day be impossible to find. Live this experience while you can; the memory will be most precious. And help preserve it for others yet to come."

The governor's letter brought a return from Hayden who responded in part: "To say the least, you have rejuvenated my faith in the politicians of our country. As I last time wrote your office with my first letter I was told by my peers that I was asking the impossible, to receive an answer to a letter sent to a politician, let alone the governor of California. And yet I did receive your letter and a remarkable one it was."

In another letter about Eureka, Reagan speaks briefly of the new practice of allowing boys to visit in the girls' dormitory. "I just wonder how long the girls are going to hold still for what must have seemed like a cute idea—the visitation rights—but now must get a little annoying when . . . they get caught half-clothed in the corridors by some joker coming to see his girlfriend."

He goes on to mention that "the Eureka of my memory was during Prohibition, but there were the same whispered words at the fraternity house about where the booze was hidden."

A letter to a fellow alumnus notes that "not too much has changed" at Eureka, "but still there is something of the characteristic so common and so disturbing in all our colleges. This generation seems to stand off with a kind of attitude of what are you going to do for me? You and I remember when we thought of the college as ours, and we involved ourselves in its problems. . . ."

And to a member of his fraternity, Tau Kappa Epsilon, he wrote, "As the years have gone by the memories I have of the four years spent in the Teke House seem to grow brighter and richer."

High school, too, holds memories that Ronald Reagan recalled in a letter to Suzy Clegg, editor of the *Scimitar* at Santana High School, Santee, California, in 1972.

". . . somehow the good memories outlast the others; for example, teachers who seemed to honestly want you to succeed and who taught you *how* to think, not *what* to think.

"I didn't study as much as I should have, and if I had it to do over I would. The extracurricular activities were a large part of my high-school life, and this I do not regret. There is much to be learned in exposing yourself to the challenges of participation. First of all, you sometimes surprise yourself with what you can do. For me athletics led the list, followed by dramatics, and last, school politics. Believe it or not I was also on the staff of the yearbook.

"In athletics, while I won letters in track and basketball, football was an all-consuming passion. It was more than a game, and most players today will admit to this. I'm glad I played and glad the game meant so much to me. There were sweet victories and heartbreaking defeats, and there were those long autumn afternoons of drill that went on into the twilight (no lights then).

"Suzy, youth is impatient and sometimes those four high-school years seem to stretch out and appear meaningless. There is an old truism that you get out of a thing only as much as you put in. If you'll permit me one line of advice—cherish these four years, participate in them to the utmost whether you are on the field or in the cheering section, selling ads in the yearbook or decorating for a party. You'll carry a treasure of memories for many years."

Letters to Ronald Reagan often strike nostalgic chords.

One letter came in asking him for a recipe his mother might have used in his childhood. "My mother has been dead for a great many years," he responded, "and I can't really recall any particular recipe. You know, back in those dark depression days . . . there was little of fancy food in our house. As a matter of fact, one of my favorites was oatmeal meat. I thought it was a luxury. Looking back I realize it was an effort to stretch hamburger by mixing oatmeal with the hamburger and then putting it in a pan and cooking it as you would hamburgers, putting gravy on it."

He adds, "If prices keep going up, it could well turn out to be the number-one recipe for almost everyone."

Books played a vital part in Reagan's early years. To Mrs. Marjorie Fluor he wrote: "I'm one of those who remembers vividly the magic of a library. Thank heaven I learned of the exciting world to be found in books and that excitement remains. No one can be lonely who has a book for company."

To S. L. Chandler of the Press Club of San Francisco, he wrote in 1968, "If one book had to be recommended or chosen for a life of exile on the proverbial island, I think the Bible would be the unquestioned choice. I know of no other book that could be read and reread and continue to be a challenge as could the Old and New Testaments.

"This, then, makes the Bible the answer to your question about a book affecting my life. I don't mean to pose as a Bible student, and perhaps it is only now in the last few years that I've recognized its effect on me. My mother was deeply religious, and my early upbringing included regular Sunday School attendance. I'm conscious now of the extent to which I was influenced by almost a kind of osmosis."

The letter also mentioned a book that as a boy he read and reread, called *Northern Trails*. It planted in him "a love of the outdoors—so deep it lasts to this day, which will come as something of a surprise to those *Chronicle* editorial writers who mistakenly think I plot the destruction of the redwoods."

Despite his love of the outdoors, one thing young Ronald Reagan was not was a hunter. His first gun, a bolt action .22, was a prize won in a swimming race. "My first hunting trip was a late November canoe trip on the Rock River in Illinois with a friend. Maybe it was the forerunner of today's survival training, but we wanted to see if we could survive overnight in the open with snow already on the ground and ice forming on the river. In early afternoon we put ashore to hunt squirrel for our evening meal.

"With the help of beginner's luck and many long hours of tin can plinking, I scored first. My reaction on bagging the squirrel [he described his first hunting trip with "my treasured rifle" in a letter to George H. Haas, senior editor of *Outdoor Life* on Aug. 10, 1976] was not one of satisfying a lust to kill. Some would have us believe this is all that motivates the hunter. The game was food; the difference between eating or going hungry on a cold winter night in the open . . . my feeling was one of accomplishment. We were faced with a necessity we lacked and we solved the problem."

In opening the letter Governor Reagan told Haas, "I am aware of the anti-hunting hysteria being generated and deplore it as you do. People must be made to understand that sportsmen today are largely responsible for the preservation of wildlife in our land."

In a letter to his former Sunday-school teacher in 1973 the governor admitted that his success sometimes seems unreal. "Every once in a while I pinch myself sitting opposite the head of state of one or other of the dozen nations we've visited, thinking this can't be 'Dutch' Reagan here. I should still be out on the dock at Lowell Park."

Show Business

WHEN RONALD REAGAN first announced his candidacy for governor, and even after his great election victory in 1966, you could hear the skeptics in both parties demean "that actor" who dared to enter politics at such a high level..

Even in 1976, ten years after his election as governor, there were those who sought to minimize his ability to govern by referring to him as a "former actor."

But why should acting be considered less serious or respectable than any other profession?

Ronald Reagan is not the first actor to rise to the governorship of a major state, although he probably is the first ever to be regarded as a serious presidential candidate.

The other actor who became governor was John Davis Lodge, a silent screen star, who was elected governor of Connecticut. Other well-known actors who have held high public office include George Murphy who was elected to the United States Senate and Helen Gahagan Douglas, who served in the House.

Former California Governor Edmund G. Brown, Sr., in his race against Reagan in 1966 probably lost many thousands of votes when a political film his campaign produced showed his telling a little black child that "You know, it was an actor who shot Lincoln."

But Ronald Reagan of Hollywood, of fifty motion pictures, of radio and television, was always much more than "just an actor." For six years of turbulence in immediate post-war Hollywood, years when the fanatical and aggressive American Communist party was actively proselytizing members throughout the industry, setting up "front" groups, and striving to become the dominant force in the industry.

In recent years efforts have been made to whitewash the Communist effort to take over the film industry with its tremendous potential to propagandize the American people. Efforts have also been made to twist and distort the role Ronald Reagan played during those difficult years.

In 1977 Governor Reagan received a detailed letter from Thomas J. Connell of New Jersey. Mr. Connell was irate about a radio broadcast he'd heard in which the commentator asserted that Reagan "had admitted to being a Communist before a Congressional Committee and 'had ratted on other Communists he knew in Hollywood.'"

Governor Reagan responded at length.

"I thank you very much for calling this to my attention. You were absolutely right; the broadcaster 100 percent wrong. Possibly he was confused, more likely deliberately so, by the fact that I have told on a number of occasions that at one time in Hollywood I found myself on the board of directors of an organization which turned out to be a communist front. I was never a communist, indeed, I was up to my neck in the fight with them when they were trying to take over Hollywood, but I have used that example to explain to audiences how many people in Hollywood were deceived by the cleverness of the communists. The finish of that story, of course, was that when I and several others like me were sure that we had been lured into what was really a front organization, we resigned and the organization without us as a cover went out of existence.

"There is a great deal of rewriting of history going on about the whole Hollywood experience. When he talks about the McCarthy blacklisting operation, he's five years out of line. I testified before the House Un-American Activities Committee, but this was in 1947. I was a friendly witness, invited by the Committee to tell what I knew of the Communist efforts in those hectic days of 1946 and

1947 when through the medium of a jurisdictional labor dispute they tried to close down and take over the entire motion picture industry. The McCarthy problems, which didn't come along until 1952, did not have to do with Hollywood but with the United States Army.

"I have been thinking of doing a book on that whole Hollywood situation simply because of the distortion of history now taking place. There was no Hollywood blacklist, in the sense that they describe it, but there were lists of names sent to Hollywood by religious groups and patriotic organizations in the country who said that they would not buy tickets to any movie in which the people on those lists appeared. We in Hollywood were able to clear some people on the lists who, as I said before, were innocently duped by the communists. We, of course, did nothing to clear those who were leaders in the effort to destroy the industry and were communists.

"The most successful blacklist in Hollywood was that of the Communists themselves who did their best to destroy the careers of people, including myself, who opposed them in what they were trying to do."

Unquestionably, show business is a more colorful, diversified industry than most. It is one in which creation of images is part of the business. But people who deal with illusion must also deal with reality, and some can deal with both very well, as Reagan watchers have found out. The people in show business, of course, are as different in character and ability as in any other segment of our society: there are the good and the bad guys, the educated and intelligent, as well as the dropouts and misfits.

I have always admired the governor for displaying nothing but pride in his former profession and calling himself fortunate for having known Hollywood during its Golden Era. He recalls incidents and people with great nostalgia and affection; his own ability and success with typical humility and frankness.

Illustrative of Reagan's deep devotion to what he always refers to as "my former profession" is a quote by the late Irvin S. Cobb, humorist, actor, columnist. Reagan quoted Cobb in a letter to Dennis R. Warren of Sacramento.

Though an inveterate stealer and rearranger of one-liners, Reagan is quick to give credit on things important. So he had no hesitancy in using Cobb to reflect his own feelings. In response to criticism of actors as being childish, Cobb wrote:

"If this be true, and if it also is true that when the curtain goes up on eternity all men must approach the gates bearing in their arms that which they have given in life, the people of show business will march in the procession carrying in their arms the pure pearl of tears, the gold of laughter, and the diamonds of stardust they spread on what might otherwise have been a rather dreary world. When at last all stand before the final stage door, I am sure the keeper will say, open, let my children in."

I can hear Ronald Reagan quoting these lines, and with a certain quiver in his voice. He is a sentimental man. But while he loves the film industry, he is not an apologist for it. And he has strong feelings about what has happened to it in recent years—the nudism, vulgarity, and pornography. He is disturbed by these things. In a letter to Lou Greenspan, executive director of the Producers Guild of America, he wrote:

"I think the industry itself has driven away a great many of its one-time constituency. I think people are tired of being embarrassed in front of their children by the new realism and I think our young people, our children, have been subverted by the current fare to where they would have to be dragged kicking and screaming in to see a picture with a G rating. Yet, the same young people, in great numbers, have discovered the old movies of the 'Golden Era' on the late television shows. While they don't realize if they have, at the same time, discovered those pictures with no four-letter words, no nude scenes, no blatant sex, no vulgarity were better theatre than today's realism. That probably brings up what is the worst sin of much of today's movie fare. It is lousy theatre.

"When did we ever get the idea that in reaching for realism we could put something on the screen that was as effective as the audience's imagination? You can't turn two people loose in bed and expect them to portray the rapture of a wedding night anywhere near as well as the audience will do it for themselves in their own imagination given just a stimulant.

"My other view is that the industry should start beating a path to Washington but not to go down the deadly road of subsidy because if you do, you'll wind up with a senior partner, headquartered in Washington.

"No, what Hollywood needs is to eliminate the court decree that separated production and exhibition. Hollywood should be allowed, like a candy store, to make the pictures in the backroom and sell them in the front. That selling can be both theatre and a form of pay television where the theatre becomes the living room—something it has already become, but for bargain-basement entertainment."

In 1971, Reagan described his feelings about Hollywood to Charles Martin:

"I came to Hollywood, a sports announcer by trade, filled with all the star-struck awe of one who had from childhood been entertained in the house of illusion—the neighborhood theatre. I never did get over being awe-struck at finding myself working with and among those familiar faces. What I remember most and what it seems to me is so lacking today is the warmth and generosity of those great stars of yesterday—their willingness to accept and include newcomers like me.

"I don't know much about modern drama schools, but they can't be better than those long hours on the set when a Pat O'Brien, a Jimmy Cagney, a Bette Davis, a Dick Powell, and a Humphrey Bogart dropped a hint here, a bit of business there, or told most entertainingly a show-business story—with a message—and beginners like me awoke one day to discover we had learned a trade.

"I'll always be grateful that I knew Hollywood in the 'Golden Era,' when it was big, brash, and confident; it could do anything and usually did. It was also the Hollywood that became Mt. Olympus for the world's theatrical skill and talent . . . an unincorporated community with a news dateline—'Hollywood.' At the same time, it was a friendly neighborhood of great warmth where the great helped the less great. Also, there was pride in craftsman-ship."

Reagan traced a little of his own Hollywood career in response to a letter asking him for help in locating some of the films in which he appeared for a Reagan Film Festival at Humboldt State College in California. He recognizes that all of his films were not classics. *Law and Order*, for in-stance, "turned out pretty bad." *Accidents Will Happen* was "just another 'B' picture . . . made prior to my own move into 'A' films."

In *Dark Victory* he had "a minor role and an unhappy experience of trying to fit myself to an interpretation dic-tated by the director and with which I was in disagreement and, frankly, unable to really meet what it was he had in mind."

International Squadron, like so many World War II films, "is hard to take after the emotionalism and the spirit of the times are taken away."

On the other hand, *Knute Rockne, All American* was a film that "marked the end of an era" for Reagan. "It really closed off all those rah rah, Joe College pictures, with the hero winning the big game, the girl, and the job all at once. From my standpoint, also, it was the part which every actor comes to at some time or other in life that marks the tran-sition into stardom.

"This was where I graduated from the 'B' pictures into subsequent films like *Kings Row*, which has been rated by some as one of the ten best pictures of all time."

But as for *The Ultimate Weapon*, it "is unknown to me; I don't know what picture that could be. It's possible the title was changed for TV distribution."

Or it's possible that some pictures are just better for-gotten. Another picture the governor always wanted to for-get was his last one, *The Killers*. He made it as a favor to a friend and in it, for the only time in his movie career, he played the bad guy. "It was a mistake," he says, making it plain that in films as in real life he prefers to wear a white hat.

Although *Kings Row* remains his personal best film, Reagan has difficulty picking out his all-time favorite. He wrote in 1971 to Carol Ann Selhorn of New Jersey: "There have been moments back through the years when I could have answered immediately, but as I try to pick one that would come to my mind I realize the theatre reflects the changing world, and what was an all-time favorite in a particular period is superseded by another with the changing times."

However, he continues, "In this era of mixed-up movies reflecting a mixed-up world, *Patton* stands out as one of the great motion picture-making jobs of this or any other time. It is unhesitating in its reflection of the brutality of war, totally honest in its probing of a man, and does this with an excellent taste which permits without offense the blunt language of the title character. It says something which needs saying today—that there are things for which men must be willing to die."

His admiration of *Patton* is unstinting. To its producer, Frank McCarthy, he wrote:

"I told you once I would hate anyone who ever played that role other than myself. Now I hate George Scott for proving that no one in the world but him could ever have played the part.

"Frank, it is a magnificent piece of picture-making and it says some things that very much need saying today. I have been greatly disturbed for sometime over the pernicious and constant degrading of the military. This picture restored a great deal of balance. I don't know whether Patton would ever be the kind of man you'd want to take on a picnic, but I do thank God that when trouble came, there were men like him around. I'm really too full of the picture yet to make specific comments other than to say it has been many years since I have so completely lost myself in a picture and have actually forgotten, while viewing it, that it was a picture. It was so real.

"I have long been an opponent, as you know, of vulgarity, obscenity, and profanity on the screen as we are seeing it in so many pictures. On the other hand, I've never believed that I was a total square and have never been opposed to the use of anything absolutely essential to the telling of the story. It did not offend me in the slightest that you had Patton talking as Patton talked. In fact, before going, I gave the Skipper quite a lecture on the man and the history surrounding him, and then told him that he would be hearing this kind of language, which didn't make it right for him or me to use, but that this was a part of the man and his character. Therefore, we sat through the movie and I had no embarrassment whatsoever about the language. It definitely belonged.

"Once again, just know that all of us were tremendously entertained and impressed, and loved every minute of the picture. Thank you for a real contribution to our nation at this time. Nancy echos and seconds all of this."

Reagan has great feelings of warmth and camaraderie, admiration, and affection for the members of his former profession. After seeing Danny Thomas in a nightclub act he wrote to him: "You were just great and I marvelled anew at your ability to take us from the sublime to the laughable and back to the sublime. It was sheer entertainment statesmanship and made me very proud.

"May I also say your courage in closing as you did was most heartwarming. I have felt for a long time that the people of our land are hungry for a return to things of the spirit. Not enough of us use our talents and our positions in testimony to God's goodness."

He reacted similarly to the film, *Kotch*, starring Jack Lemmon and Walter Matthau. To Lemmon he wrote: "A few days ago flying to Washington I was one of a group of airborne at about 39,000 feet who must have been the happiest humans on or above the earth. You and Walter Matthau were responsible for this. For a few hours we watched your picture, *Kotch*.

"Jack, it was a pure delight, and I resolved as I took off the headphones to write you and also Walter, which I am doing, to tell you what a great joy it was to see real pros at work. If ever there was a two-man tour de force, this was it. I'll be seeing it again, because I want Nancy to see it, although I've described every foot of film to her.

"Please don't take it easy—keep on working and doing jobs like this one. You are needed by a great many people."

He sent a copy of that letter to Matthau with an added

paragraph that read: "I have to add, just for you, your portrayal of an elderly man was so great, so perfect, that I'm sure every actor had the same reaction as I did, that little uncertain question in the mind, 'Could I ever do such a job?' I'm afraid for most of us the answer is no. It's been a long time since I hated to see a picture come to an end, but on this one I wanted you to keep right on going and visit the young lady, drop in on your son for Christmas, and I wanted to watch you do it all for as long as that airplane would stay up there."

Unable to attend a dinner honoring Jimmy Durante, he sent a letter which read, in part: "Jimmy, if giving people pleasure and the gift of laughter were measured in gold, you would have given away a billion dollars. A few in our business earn the distinction of being called a 'legend in their own time.' You are among that few. You never got laughs by hurting or embarrassing anyone, your humor had heart, warmth, and kindness. You are in more hearts than you will ever know. May the road rise beneath your feet and the wind be always at your back."

Time after time he is asked to comment on actors he has known. Without exception, his words are kindly and gracious. About Errol Flynn he wrote: "Sometimes I could get so mad at him I wanted to hit him over the head with a camera. At the same time I felt a great tragedy surrounded him. Physically he was a magnificent piece of machinery. He could have been a fantastic athlete in almost any sport. In acting, of course, this gave him grace in action beautiful to behold. He was one of the few in our profession who could truly take the romantic roles in the costume epics and look the part so believably. He had total audience acceptance. This became evident in his few attempts at straight roles in modern clothes. While he wanted to do this, I always felt he lost some inner confidence when he was without the trappings of the costume pictures.

"The sense of tragedy I mentioned was because with all this going for him he had no confidence in his acting ability. He was fearful of competition from others in his own pictures. The result was [that] many times he would try to get script alterations taking advantage of his star power and influence to lessen some other actor's part in the picture. This is the point at which you wanted to hit him over the head with a camera. He really could hold his own. He had a commanding presence on screen. If he had only known his own capacity he would have realized how much better his scenes and the picture could have been if he had allowed the rest of the cast to help play and build those scenes.

"Errol was one of the most instantly likeable people I have ever met. He had great charm. Somehow I feel the problems besetting him in his private life stemmed from the same insecurity he felt in his profession.

"I'm glad I knew him and glad I had the opportunity to be in two pictures with him. I only wish somehow someone had been able to show him how little he had to fear and how really great he could have become. There is no one in the business now quite like him."

He told of his admiration for Barbara Stanwyck in a letter to Miss Ella Smith, assistant professor of dramatic arts at the University of Connecticut: *"Cattle Queen of Montana* was the only picture I ever made with Barbara Stanwyck, although I have known her for many years. She is one of the best thought-of and most respected performers in all the industry.

"Working with her I discovered why. She is a pro. Her only intolerance is of those who won't take our profession seriously, and who come to work without their lines learned or who are late and careless in their work. She is ready every day exactly on time, her lines learned perfectly for each day's shooting, prepared to undergo whatever had to be done to make the scene better for the audience who will eventually see the movie.

"In *Cattle Queen* for example, there is a scene where she is bathing in a mountain lake. The director was prepared to shoot this with a double because the temperature of the water was in the mid-forties. Naturally, the scene would not be as good if the camera had had to play far enough away for use of a double. She insisted on doing the scene herself. She is most helpful to other performers, sacrificing many times some personal advantage in the scene and throwing the scene to another when she thinks it will benefit the overall story.

"You asked about the S.A.G. [Screen Actors Guild] award. Nothing illustrates more her personality and attitude. Those who knew her were concerned that if she suspected she was getting an award she wouldn't be there, so they invited her to come down and present the award to me. She was standing offstage, fully expecting to come out and make the presentation of the first such award to me, when she heard me making the presentation to her."

Both Reagan and Boris Karloff were active in the Screen Actors Guild "back in those dark days after World War II when we met for so many long hours each day to try and keep the studios open in the face of the communist-inspired attempt through labor troubles to dominate the industry."

To an acquaintance seeking anecdotes for a book about Karloff, he wrote that "I have only the warmest memories of him," adding, "Boris was one of the warmest, kindest, most gentle human beings I have ever met, and at all times a perfect gentleman. He was modest and unassuming and, yet, in his quiet way, contributed so much in our deliberations. He had great, good common sense plus a sense of fairness typical of his great integrity. Nancy was on the board in those days and both of us held him in such great affection that love is the only word I can use to describe him.

"I left out one other descriptive word. When the stories would lead into banter and joking, he also had a most delightful sense of humor. I'm sorry I can't recall some specific incident that would be of use to you. I can only say that many a time I would find myself looking at him and wondering how this kindly man fell into the type-casting of monsters and villains. He was the complete opposite of the parts he played."

Though he did not know Audie Murphy well, he took the death of the famed World War II Medal of Honor winner and postwar actor hard. After Murphy's death in an airplane crash he wrote a letter to Mrs. Murphy, which like so many of his letters, reflects his strong faith in God. It read in part:

"When tragedy strikes we inevitably ask why, and, of course, there is no answer. But of one thing I'm sure: our lives have a purpose known only to God, and God had a plan for Audie Murphy which was not completed with his magnificent wartime service.

"Perhaps the fulfillment of that purpose is yet to come in the lives of Audie's sons. If that is so, then you are a very great part of God's plan. I know this is a difficult time for young people to see heroism in any act associated with war, and that is too bad. Some men will go through life and never find themselves in a position where they are the only ones who can do the dirty job that has to be done. Some will face such a moment and fail. Some, like Audie, accept and do the dirty job because there is no one else there to do it, and they know in their hearts it must be done. Your sons should be aware, and no doubt are, of what not only a nation, but civilization itself owes to men like their father."

At Peace with the Press

RONALD REAGAN IS an expert in dealing with members of the news media. He is comfortable with them, and I think one can safely say that with a few exceptions he is well liked by them.

Considering the press's function, I think it's impossible for any public official to have more than a mutually respectful relationship with the press. It is unfortunate, however, when that relationship deteriorates to prejudice or outright hostility on either side. With both having such distinct and different areas of responsibility to the public, theoretically, they should be able to work for the common good. That it doesn't always work out that way is due to a variety of reasons on both sides.

One of the more serious reasons is the decline of professionalism among some newsmen. No longer do many of them consider objectivity essential. Those who embrace the "new journalism" no longer seem willing to leave opinion to the columnists and editorial writers. These reporters prejudge events according to their prejudices, and their news stories reflect their failure to get all the facts. You don't have to be a politician to be upset if you find yourself the victim of sloppy reporting or misrepresentation, but those in public office seem all too often to be the chief victims.

On the other side of the coin, public officials too often

expect confirmation and justification of their words and actions in the media, forgetting that the media's job is to question, to report, and to criticize if criticism is called for. There have been countless instances where the press has exposed deplorable situations which would otherwise have gone unnoticed and unremedied.

A case is that of the lone and courageous reporter for the *Sacramento Union* who disclosed the outrageous benefits California's legislators had voted themselves at taxpayer expense.

This reporter succeeded in arousing the public to such an extent that the legislature was forced to rescind its pork-barrel actions. This, of course, is just a small example of the benefits of a free press; no one will argue that it is not one of the foundations of our country's freedom.

But we can rely on it only if its members perform in the highest tradition of their profession. What happens if they don't report accurately or completely or honestly? What recourse does the public or the office holder have if they report some stories and not others?

I have read that a major TV network devoted more reporting time to trivial matters than to our nation's defense system which has dangerously declined in recent years. Is that a responsible free press, deserving of our trust and confidence?

We must always be just a little suspicious of whatever we read. I have been witness to too many examples of inaccurate or biased reporting. And sadly, once the damage is done, no letter to the editor or retraction on some inside page of the paper can ever undo the damage or change the opinions created by one false headline or one misstatement of fact.

Kim Marcus, a reporter for the Skyline College Press in San Bruno, California, was not the first reporter to make one particular false assumption, then write it. Miss Marcus, covering a speech by Governor Reagan before the Commonwealth Club in San Francisco on January 18, 1978, wrote that Reagan's face "was applied with heavy amounts of 'pancake' makeup . . ."

Had Miss Marcus checked, instead of assuming, she

would have learned that Governor Reagan never wears makeup, not even on television, nor did he as an actor. Any former member of his staff, any reporter who has covered him regularly, knows that.

Her article brought from the governor a letter to the editor of the college paper in which he said that Miss Marcus "did manage to touch a nerve when she described my face as 'applied with heavy amounts of pancake makeup.' I didn't wear any makeup when I was in movies and doing television.

"Please tell Miss Marcus that I wore no makeup at the Commonwealth Club (I'm allergic to it). In the interest of press integrity also tell her she has a standing invitation to do a 'white glove' test on my face the next time she is assigned to cover an appearance of mine!"

Governor Reagan has made similar offers to reporters who think he dyes his hair or has had a face lift. Neither is true. I know.

The governor touched on the press's ability to do harm in a letter to Maxwell H. Smith of Malibu, California: "I very much fear the press contributes to divisiveness in our country by printing stories and ignoring their responsibility to check out the facts themselves. They justify this by saying, 'well, if some prominent individual makes a charge, that charge becomes news.' But can they really absolve themselves from a responsibility as an information agency to editorially present the facts on the other side? Perhaps this is one reason why a great many American institutions are today so suspect."

Governor Ronald Reagan probably spent more time than he should have trying to set the record straight on such sensitive issues as education and mental health when his administration was victimized in the press. Unfortunately, his efforts seldom seem to have reached the public. Not surprisingly, press misrepresentation on personal matters also annoyed him.

In a letter to William F. Buckley, Jr., of *National Review,* he alluded to an exchange of published letters between Buckley and Abe Rosenthal, managing editor of the *New*

York Times, letters in which Reagan and Rosenthal made factual errors. The letter reads:

"I was cleaning a few stacks of correspondence away on my desk, and came upon your letters to Mr. Rosenthal of the *Times* and his letter to you. I had kept all this because I enjoy reading Buckley—Mr. Rosenthal I can take or leave alone.

"Looking at his letter again, however, I realize he shot a few arrows into the air, and you had never been provided (by me) with a tracking device to determine how far off course his little arrows were.

"Arrow number one had to do with our residence and the old 'mansion.' He says Nancy declared it a fire trap and moved out, and wealthy friends bought a house which we rented at twelve hundred dollars per month. At the end of a year the state kindly took it over; thus rent now becomes income. All because we could not go back to living in the 'old mansion.'

"The state fire marshal declared the 'old mansion' a fire-trap long before we moved in. We moved out after a fire scare which served to remind us we had an eight-year-old nesting about thirty feet above the ground. Wealthy friends did not immediately buy a house for us to rent. We rented from a native Sacramentan, who subsequently put the house up for sale at the request of the Internal Revenue Service, who had him on the cuff for about half a million in unpaid taxes. We searched the town for another house to rent, and were within two weeks of being evicted as our unsuccessful search went on.

"It was at this point a group of citizens (some friends and some men we'd never met who are stalwart Democrats) bought the house and took over the lease. We continued paying the rent for about three years. As the 1970 election drew near, my opponent began a campaign of innuendos that somehow, by paying my own rent, I was beholden to 'half-hidden millionaires' who were my landlords. The California Constitution requires the state to provide a governor's residence. The 'old mansion' has long since been taken over by Parks and Recreation, and it is a tourist attraction. Please note, tourists are not allowed above the ground floor, due to the fire hazard. So a year ago I told the legislature I was fed up with all the hanky-panky, and the state could damn well take over paying the rent, thereby severing any supposed umbilical cord between me and the landlords."

In the same letter Reagan unhesitatingly lashes a *Times* article on his tax troubles. He goes on, "Now since the *Times* saw fit to pursue my tax matter—all the way to having someone pose as a cattle buyer visiting ranches and sniffing around for a Reagan brand, all of which resulted in a *Times* Sunday feature as dishonest as the *Times* could make it— I'll spoil his martini with a fact or two.

"My continuing interest in cattle and ranching did not produce the tax shelter his paper alleged. My total investment in breeding bulls was ten thousand dollars, which doesn't buy many cattle at today's prices. I regularly receive ordinary income from that investment which I dutifully declare.

"The mystery of my evil loopholes is somewhat reduced when you consider that two very legitimate items alone, namely 'other taxes' (deductible for purposes of computing income tax under California and federal laws) and contributions to church and charity, totaled almost half my gross salary as governor.

"By the way, 'when the roll is called up yonder,' do you think not paying a tax you don't owe will rate as many demerits as receiving stolen property and selling it for profit? Maybe that is oversimplification, but somehow in my mind it applies to the *Times* and the purloined [Pentagon] papers."

Misinformation released by the media often resulted in a flood of letters to the governor either criticizing him or asking him to explain. The tax story triggered one such flood, since many newspaper stories never made it clear that he had not evaded his state taxes; he merely did not owe any. Some liberal newspapers editorialized against him, implying that he had evaded his taxes and should have paid something.

Ignored by most of the press was the principle of tax paying laid down by the famous liberal judge, Learned

Hand. Hand wrote that "there is nothing sinister in so arranging one's affairs as to keep taxes just as low as possible.
Nobody owes any public duty to pay more than the law
demands. Taxes are enforced exactions, not voluntary contributions. To demand more in the name of morals is mere
cant."

In a letter about his taxes and misrepresentation of the
situation not only in the press but in the classroom, Reagan
explained: "I cannot tell you how much I appreciate your
writing to me and giving me a chance to hopefully straighten
the record on the misinformation you received in the classroom.

"Your story is not an unfamiliar one. I have come to the
conclusion that much of the dissatisfaction, the mistrust of
all our established institutions, is being fostered in too many
social studies courses.

"As you perhaps know, through all my years in pictures
I had as a sideline, in fact a sideline which was my main
interest, ranching. It was a small operation, breeding horses
and raising some cattle, and certainly I never could have
lived on the basis of my success as a rancher. I was unable
to continue actively in that sideline activity when I became
governor. Disposing of the ranch, but wanting to at least
have a feeling of still being active in agriculture, I invested
a relatively small amount of money in breeding bulls
through a company which handles the business end of putting those bulls out on lease on a number of ranches throughout the country. Last year, when the furor arose over the
fact that last year I had no state income tax obligation, the
New York Times went out of its way to publish the fact that
I had this cattle investment. They made it seem as if it was
a tremendous, Texas-size, operation, and then falsely stated
that it was a tax device and probably the reason I had no
income tax obligation. They charged the old demagogic
thing of some kind of loophole. The truth is, my modest
investment of a few thousand dollars in a small herd of
bulls actually contributed a few dollars of income I had to
declare. I had a small profit, less than a few hundred dollars
over and above the expense of keeping the bulls.

"Since this whole thing was tied into the matter of my

state income tax, perhaps I should give you in advance some information on that. First of all, this was the first time such a thing had ever happened to me, and it was purely the result of my transition from the television industry which, obviously, paid several times more than does the job of governor. Naturally, there were many things I could not shift immediately, responsibilities to charities I had previously supported, etc., in those first few years in office, so my tax situation was rather up and down. For example, the year before I had no tax obligation to the state, my income tax was more than double my total salary as governor. I am sure the teacher would be happy to know that this year I have paid a normal state income tax.

"To sum up, you can inform this teacher that I have no subsidies from government of any kind. I own a small number of bulls; I board them out and pay their board at a variety of ranches and, at the end of the year, they deliver a few dollars in additional income."

The governor's embarrassment and anger at the rash of misleading stories on his tax situation were matched only by the embarrassment of the reporter who asked the question that brought the reply that, no, the governor had paid no state income tax for the year 1970.

Perhaps I should give a little background here. Income tax returns in California, like federal tax returns, are confidential. It is a felony for a state employee to divulge them. Yet one state employee who saw the governor's tax returns passed the word to a college radio-station reporter that the governor had paid no taxes.

The script of the college reporter's almost unnoticed broadcast was then passed to the members of the Sacramento press corps. The person who asked the question of the governor, a careful and accurate reporter, was dismayed at the outcry that resulted. He wrote to the governor: "The stories that resulted—like so many—[were] blown all out of proportion. A curiosity item dwelling upon vindictive reaction to your own personal financial misfortune—trivia when compared to the problems of the state and the suggested solutions.

"For my part, for your embarrassment I am truly sor-

rowful. For the personal difficulty it has caused you I shall
be eternally sorry."

Reagan responded: "Nancy and I were both happy to
receive your letter and want you to know we had already
been informed that you were not the plant who was supposed
to ask the question.

"We understood your motive in asking. Don't feel bad
about it because someone else would have asked, and probably with the same result.

"Have no fear with regard to our friendship: we still
value it very highly."

Reagan also responded to what probably is a classic story
of how innaccuracies printed and reprinted by the press
become conventional truths in the eyes of both the press
and the public when a generally respected capitol reporter
started a story that began, "With Spiro T. Agnew gone from
the public scene, Governor Reagan has emerged as perhaps
the nation's most controversial figure of speech." He re-
counted some Reagan "bloopers" without putting them in
the context of the time, place, and situation where they
were said. More in an effort to set the record straight than
in anger, Reagan wrote the following letter to him.

"I couldn't help but drop you a note regarding your recent
story in the Sunday *Sacramento Union*. You know I'm not
given to railing at the press but in this instance I do feel
justified in pointing out that the overall effect your story
gives of putting my foot in my mouth is based less on what
I've said than on what someone else has accused me of
saying.

"I'm sure you are not guilty of deliberate distortion but
have only accepted the oft-repeated version of the incidents
you used as gospel. If so, it is a case of journalism feeding
on original journalistic errors.

"Sometimes I'm reminded of all the Jimmy Cagney im-
itators who inevitably wind up saying in Cagney style, 'you
dirty rat,' until everyone believes that it is a classic line
from one of his movies. The truth is, Jimmy never spoke
the line in his entire life.

"Let's take my supposed use of the term 'blood bath.'
Yes, I used the words but not in the way one, and I em-

phasize, *one* reporter carried them. Others of the press covering the meeting found no news in the statement nor was there any until one reporter put the words in a context completely different from the way they were used.

"Officials of the University of California who are not usually hesitant to criticize me were present at the meeting and were high in their approval of what I'd said. Perhaps (as I've said since) a more apt figure of speech might have been, 'bite the bullet.' At any rate, 'blood bath' was *never* used in the sense of encouraging violence on the campus in those troubled times—actually the very opposite was intended.

"You did correct the wording of the 'redwood' line but still used it as an illustration of a political slip of the tongue. Frankly, I'd use it again because I was talking about the pride Californians should feel about the way we have saved our redwood trees. It certainly was not a remark indicating callous disregard for the redwoods. But again, one reporter *re*-interpreted and my opponent in the campaign took off with it.

"As for the most recent remark and the one which evidently prompted your story—you know how careful I've been to avoid any statement that might endanger Patty Hearst. How many private conversations have you been in where speculation, theorizing, and even outright cracks have been made, none of which you would make public in a news story? Possibly I'm denied that right, but I can't help but feel that (again) the *one* reporter who heard of my remark secondhand and *made* a story of it was guilty of an even greater irresponsibility. And frankly, my attempt to level with all of you in the press corps was used by many in a way that revealed a total lack of concern for Patty's safety.

"'No comment' is becoming a more attractive refuge every day but I'd hate to use it because it would be of little benefit to the people of California.

"I hope you accept this in the way it is intended. It was written only because we have had a relationship I value."

The reporter responded, "I appreciate your note of March 14 and the thought that went into it.

"There certainly was no attempt to deliberately distort your comments. Our credibility, both with news sources and with our public readership, is vital to the survival of a free press.

"Yes, statements once reported—regardless of degree of accuracy and context—sometimes become etched in granite. It is the duty of a professional, fair-minded reporter to make certain the basic facts were accurate, as well as providing a complete frame of reference for those facts."

On a lighter note he promised "never to write that *Bedtime for Bonzo* was the pinnacle of your screen career."

The governor's letters in seeking to set the record straight often referred to the *New York Times* which, while it may run "all the news that's fit to print" does not always do so accurately. In one case a Connecticut teacher wrote the governor because "my students have asked me to write to you about the enclosed article from the *New York Times*." The article dealt with remarks the governor had made concerning those involved in Watergate. Though it ran in the *Times* the article was filed out of Sacramento by United Press International (UPI). The first two paragraphs read, "Governor Ronald Reagan said yesterday that the Watergate spies should not be considered criminals because they are not criminals at heart.

"Mr. Reagan, who espouses a strict law-and-order philosophy, conceded that the electronic bugging of the Democratic party headquarters was illegal but said 'criminal' was too harsh a term to use."

The teacher wrote of his students: "They are confused. Briefly, what they want to know is: If a poor man breaks into a supermarket and steals food to feed his family, is he a 'criminal' or is he an 'illegal'? If a businessman hires someone to break into his competitor's office and steal a secret process, is he a 'criminal' or an 'illegal'? If a politician hires someone to break into his opponent's office to steal information that will help elect him and his associates into offices worth millions of dollars, is he a 'criminal' or an 'illegal'?

"Ordinarily I would not have paid too much attention to these queries. But, 1) I can't answer them; and 2) these children are the sons and daughters of American executives and government officials who will inherit the sort of job that you have. They are mostly Republicans and they want an explanation. I believe they have a point. I hope you will give them a personal and responsive answer."

Reagan's reply: "I am delighted to have the opportunity to answer your students' questions and congratulate them for their perception and their concern.

"Part of my happiness in answering is because it gives me a chance to point out the distortions which have become so commonplace in recent years in press coverage particularly where public figures are concerned. In the case of the *New York Times* story the distortion is one of omission and slanting to get exactly the tone that prompted you to write.

"I realize the press cannot devote unlimited space to carry, for example, a rather lengthy conversation (which this was) but it is nevertheless improper to alter the gist of that conversation so as to provide a headline, 'Reagan says spies are not criminals.'

"Of course the breaking and entering of the Watergate headquarters was both a criminal act and an illegal act. The hypothetical case of the poor man stealing food for his family was likewise criminal and illegal. In our system of justice allowance is made, however, for extenuating circumstances. Any court would deal differently in the case of the poor man stealing food and the businessman attempting to steal business secrets for personal gain.

"In my conversation with the reporters I had remarked about the great human tragedy involved in Watergate; that campaign tactics have for many years had a kind of 'fraternity initiation' atmosphere where both sides expect shenanigans. In this context I pointed out that none of the men had criminal natures and probably wouldn't ever intentionally double park, but now their lives could very well be ruined and a number will undoubtedly go to prison for something done in the emotionalism of a political campaign, and which none of them thought of as criminal. Do college students think of themselves as criminals when they go from one campus to another to steal a statue or historic bell prior to the big game? But they are stealing.

"In my conversation I made it clear the guilty should be punished, and I expressed a hope that possibly we'd all review our attitude toward campaign hooliganism in the future. I do take issue with you that offices are sought because they are worth millions of dollars. If monetary gain were the reason, then I would have stayed in TV where I was earning roughly five times my present salary as governor.

"But referring back to campaign hooliganism [may I remind you that] Senator McGovern stated publicly he knew Watergate was a Republican caper because his informant in the Nixon headquarters told him it was. In Kansas, according to a news story, his staff happily boasted of breaking and entering to get party membership lists they weren't supposed to have during the primary. Ellsberg, now freed on a technicality, confessed to stealing the Pentagon papers because he felt the end justified the means. Columnist Jack Anderson printed transcripts from the grand jury and refused to identify his source, although taking such transcripts is a felony. Ralph Nader has urged industrial employees to steal and to provide him with information from their employers' files.

"All of these things are wrong. All are technically criminal and illegal. How many of us in hearing them mentally made allowance for some or all? But the truth is, Watergate can't be wrong and Ellsberg right.

"There is a great need for all of us to stop short, take inventory, and see if we don't need a return to the ethics of an earlier day when personal honor enjoyed a higher status than we've been giving it. We can have human compassion for those who slip, but we can also demand personal accountability.

"What has been happening to our society has been a gradual and insidious thing. It includes, if you will, our acceptance of the intentional foul in basketball. If an opponent by good playing has moved into position for a sure shot is it right to foul him and rob him of the reward he's entitled to?

"Watergate will serve a useful purpose if all of us will decide that law and order begins with each one of us."

One of the early controversies of the Reagan administration was the firing by the Board of Regents of the University of California of University President Clark Kerr. This was in February 1967.

Additionally there was ongoing controversy between Governor Reagan and the university for almost the entire eight years of his governorship. In March of 1972 the governor wrote to the editor of the UCLA *Daily Bruin* in an effort to correct statements and innuendoes Kerr made in an interview with a *Daily Bruin* reporter.

"In your March 1 issue, you carried a story by one of your staff writers, Dave McNary, containing an interview with former U.C. President Clark Kerr. I'm sure Mr. McNary wrote in good faith and with complete confidence in the answers provided by Dr. Kerr. My letter is prompted by the rewriting of history which took place in that article and which gave at least a chilling reminder of *1984*.

"First of all, to refer to the campus turmoil between 1964 and 1967 as 'peaceful nonviolent affairs' is like calling the Johnstown Flood a backed-up drain. All through the 1965 gubernatorial campaign, wherever my opponent or I appeared, the people had one thing uppermost in their minds: the question would be shouted in chorus, 'What are you going to do about Berkeley?' Neither Governor Brown nor I could seek this job without recognizing something had to be done.

"The clear impression is given by Dr. Kerr that I succeeded in firing him at the first regents' meeting I attended three weeks after my inauguration. It is time the truth is put on record. At my first regents' meeting, routine business was conducted for some hours. When we went into executive session late in the afternoon, I wasn't aware that two of the regents and Clark Kerr were not in their places until the two regents returned, visibly upset. They announced that Dr. Kerr had called them into his office to deliver an ultimatum. He told them he was aware of the two years of strained relations with the board and he could not continue under such circumstances; therefore, he demanded a vote of confidence from the board—that day—or he would resign. One regent said that perhaps the board should give in because to do otherwise might be embarrassing to me. Until then, I hadn't participated in any of the board's discussions, but now I told them they had no right to make a decision involving the university based on its possible effect in Sacramento. They should do what they believed was best for the university. On a roll-call vote, the ultimatum was rejected.

"As for the rest of the rewritten history, Angela Davis, after public declaration that she was not just a communist, in the sense of subscribing to that philosophy but was a member of the American Communist Party, was ordered dismissed. The regents had no choice . . . the university itself had a rule on the books that no one could be hired to teach who was a member of that party *or any other organization* whose tenets restricted freedom of thought. A court order cancelled the dismissal, but the university told us she had been hired for one year only and would not be rehired when the year was up.

"One last thing: budgets. The university administration has used the phrase 'budget cuts' over and over again until, like 'newsspeak,' there is widespread belief that we did indeed reduce existing budgets. This is patently false. During my administration, enrollment at the university had increased 35.4 percent; state financial support for the university had increased 56.8 percent. That should answer two more discrepancies—one, that the university has quit growing and, two, that we have reduced support.

"May I take the liberty of suggesting that you of the *Daily Bruin* have a great opportunity to advance the cause of truth. Don't believe what you are told without checking to see if there is another side—and that goes for what I've just written. Check me out."

Many of the governor's letters to members of the press were meant not only to set the record straight but also to inform and educate. A letter to a California columnist on the complicated subject of tax reform provides a good example.

"I read with great interest your column (May 19), 'We Can't Stand More Tax Relief.' As you can imagine, I' not in agreement with a number of your conclusions.

"It is true that our tax reform proposal this time and for the first time contains an increase over and above the shift of property tax to other tax sources. However, that increase is not a 'slick' way of augmenting the state's take from the taxpayer. The increase is earmarked for public schools and represents a necessary response to the Serrano opinion of the Supreme Court.

"Another element of our proposal, the increase of the 'automobile in-lieu tax' goes entirely to city, county, and local schools in equal shares. This was done to compensate in part for our insistence that property taxes, once reduced remain frozen at that level.

"In your comparison of our proposal with the Moretti plan you suggested that ours was a greater burden to the 'little guy.' Since his plan raises income taxes eight hundred million dollars and ours reduces them slightly and his plan includes an actual net tax increase more than five times as great as ours, I have to disagree with your conclusion.

"Finally you say, 'The fact remains the state is short of the money it wants and the taxpayers are going to come up with it somehow.' In the last five and one-half years, the state has returned directly to the taxpayers more than two billion dollars. There was the one-time ten percent rebate on income tax, the twenty percent rebate this year, the seventy-dollar rebate to homeowners a few years ago and the seven hundred and fifty-dollar property-tax exemption. The state pays local government several hundred million dollars each year to make up for this reduction in local property tax revenue.

"Incidentally, while our proposal contains a certain amount of new money for schools, if federal revenue sharing is adopted, we will be able to offer the taxpayers an across-the-board cut in state income taxes at the same time we increase state aid for schools.

"Most of the increase in the state budget is in the two-thirds of the budget which is returned to local government. We actually run the state, including the University of California and the state colleges plus highway construction and all the other state functions, on one-third of the total state budget. And we have fewer employees than we had five years ago. Of the citizen's tax dollar, running the state takes less than seven cents. The federal government takes about sixty-five cents and local government and schools use thirty cents. If real savings are to be made for the taxpayer, they can be made by citizens paying closer attention to how their money is spent in their own communities and by Uncle Sam in Washington. If the state closed down our great universities and colleges entirely the taxpayer would only get a reduction of less than one and one-half cents on the dollar. May I suggest there are better pickings for the tax payer than Sacramento.

"Someday, why don't you pay us a visit and let us lay out the whole complicated matter for you? Frankly, we think there is money to be saved in government and you could be of help."

A letter to Brigadier General James F. Hamlet, commander of the First Cavalry Division's Third Brigade, alludes to what Reagan, along with many other Americans, thought was biased television coverage of the war in Vietnam:

"Dear General Hamlet:

"Some time ago you evidently challenged a CBS correspondent to go with you in your helicopter to visit the Third Brigade, First Cavalry Division, where they were engaged with the enemy. Recently the film taken of this visit was played here in the states on CBS News. May I say it was a most refreshing change from the usual CBS war coverage. I couldn't help but write and tell you how very proud you made a great many of us. Your remarks in your interview and the remarks of your men made us realize how deeply indebted we are to people like you who are doing so much in behalf of freedom for all of us."

The governor's older daughter, Maureen, has also felt the slings and arrows of an inaccurate press. Maureen complained in a letter to the editor of the *San Diego Union*, a copy of which she sent to her father, that "your newspaper printed an account" of a speech she had given "which is a complete distortion of my views. . . ."

Her father responded in a philosophical vein: "Based on my own experience I wouldn't suggest you hold your breath until you get the retraction or apology." He added, "If it will help any, let me just say that I'm sure you are overly concerned about how many might see it and possibly be offended. They'll probably never see it. I am amazed at how little most people do read the papers or even remember the stories. I know we all assume that, because it's there and because we saw it, everyone has read it. But I'm afraid most people scan the headlines, turn to the stock report, the sport page, or the comics, and that's it. So don't lose any sleep over what happened."

An Eye on the Horizon

I FEEL SORRY for any man occupying a governor's chair without holding his own deep-seated personal philosophy. For every governor is faced with a multitude of grave problems, each of which seems to have legitimate and persuasive arguments for and against each possible solution. These are presented forcefully, and often directly, to the governor, by the proponents and opponents of each issue, including legislators, lobbyists, special interest groups, and news media.

Under this barrage where does the sincere, honest chief executive find his answer if not within himself? When the temptation to make a political decision, instead of going with the right decision regardless of politics, becomes ever so attractive, as it sometimes does, strength of character, supported by strong personal convictions and ideals is desperately needed.

The decision-making process varies from administration to administration. I have been told that former Governor Edmund G. (Pat) Brown did not have a hard and fast system. He left it up to his department heads to come to him with problems they couldn't solve. Brown had about forty department heads reporting directly to him.

Our administration was never a rudderless ship. Shortly after entering office, Ronald Reagan established the semiweekly cabinet sessions as the vehicle he would use to keep abreast of the state's problems. Attending these meetings were the four agency administrators, the director of finance, the Republican constitutional officers, as well as his own top-level staff.

In California the statewide constitutional officers are the governor, the lieutenant governor, the secretary of state, the controller, the treasurer, the attorney general, and the superintendent of public instruction. During Reagan's first term all but the attorney general were Republicans. In his second term all were Republicans except the secretary of state and the superintendent of public instruction.

Governor Reagan reorganized the government within weeks after his swearing in. He set up four cabinet-level agencies, each headed by a secretary. These were the secretaries of Business and Transportation, Agriculture and Services, Resources, and Health and Welfare.

The cabinet meeting format resembled board of directors meetings in that every issue was "round-tabled" and everyone had his say. The major difference was that there was no vote taken at the end. It was the governor alone who made the final decision on each issue, based, of course, on all the information he had received.

Obviously, not all problems could be settled with one discussion. Some issues were discussed in as many as thirty or forty meetings. On other occasions the governor would request a period for quiet contemplation. He would take the problem home and do his soul-searching at night. Whatever the outcome, it was always the result of his convictions, backed by the courage to carry out what he felt was right.

That courage was renewed constantly by the governor's strong faith in the Lord. In a letter to an old friend, the Reverend Ben H. Cleaver of Cape Girardeau, Missouri, in May of 1971, he wrote,

"I am very grateful today for a faith in which you played a part in instilling within me. The Lord sometimes must tire of hearing me ask Him for strength, courage, and wisdom. I couldn't attempt this job for one day without His help."

The letter was one expressing general frustration with both the legislature and the bureaucracy. Of the legislature he wrote, "We are into what should be the closing weeks of the session with absolutely nothing accomplished. Fortunately, in their obstructionism and hostility, they have made serious political mistakes. . . .

"Now they are attempting to hold up legislation and the budget until they can force me to join them in announcing the need for a tax increase because they realize they've put themselves in an untenable position with the public. . . .

"If I have to admit to the need for tax increase, I will only do so because, having secured welfare reform and having reduced the budget as far as is humanly possible, the revenues are still insufficient and are needed to avoid deficit. I absolutely refuse to support a tax increase for new or additional spending."

Returning to welfare reform, he wrote that "about a year ago I appointed a task force, including citizens from the community as well as people in government, to review the entire ridiculous welfare structure. I think we are the only state that has finally compiled the information we have and most of my fellow governors are coming to us for that information."

Then he turned to his dealings with the bureaucracy. "I have kicked the bureaucracy in the shins, and I am discovering how great can be their resentment. They have a very tight union. There occurs even sabotage within our own state government from those in the permanent structure who think elected representatives are only temporary and, therefore, to be ignored. I understand better the meaning of the poignant lines written by Whittaker Chambers when he turned away from communism. He said, 'When I took up my little bow and aimed at communism, I also hit something else. What I hit was that socialist revolution which, under the name of liberalism, has been inching its ice cap over the world and this nation for the past twenty years. I knew of its existence, but I was totally unprepared for its extent, the depth of its revolutionary anger.'"

Tax problems, in all their ramifications, were always present during the Reagan years in Sacramento. Despite never-ending efforts to "squeeze, cut, and trim" every possible ounce of fat out of state government, inflation, federally mandated programs, special needs, and efforts to limit local property taxes drove state spending up every year.

Glib spenders early called on the governor to institute a withholding program for state income-tax collections similar to the federal government's withholding program as a way of easing the burden. They said the program would not only bring in extra money but would also help the state's chronic cash flow problem.

The governor held out as long as he could, proclaiming that "my feet are in concrete" on the issue of withholding. His philosophy was that withholding made taxes too easy to pay because people didn't miss money taken out of their pay checks. "Taxes should hurt" he said, so that taxpayers would be *aware* of them and pressure their legislators to hold taxes down.

The phrase "taxes should hurt" came back to haunt Governor Reagan many times as editorial writers, columnists, and others deliberately twisted the remark to mean that he was heartless and cruel, and didn't care if people had to scrimp to pay their taxes. That, of course, wasn't—and isn't—the case at all. Few governors have cared as much for all the people and none has worked as hard as Ronald Reagan to keep taxes under control.

In a letter to Caspar Weinberger, then chairman of the Federal Trade Commission, but previously the state finance director, the governor explained that, "The deciding factor, however, had nothing to do with that, nor have I changed my mind about the philosophy back of the system, but the increase in the income tax wouldn't solve our cash-flow problem which is getting very acute. I just saw no other way out. Some of our hard-nosed friends are, of course, very resentful. However, one plus is that our most recent surveys and the polls we've been quietly taking, as you know, reveal that beginning last May, there was a strange shift in sentiment and the majority was for withholding. My own interpretation is that probably last April was the first time people felt the full impact of the '67 tax increase, and I've had individuals contact me who agree with me philosophically but who have said they need the convenience that it offers. Several legislators have come to me and told me that their districts previously against have, by way of polls in their newsletters, undergone the same change.

"The tremors from the cracking of concrete around my feet must have been felt in Washington."

The mention of cracking concrete referred to his earlier statement that his feet were in concrete. When he announced to the press his decision to endorse withholding he did it with the jocular remark that "That sound you hear is the concrete cracking around my feet." Later, members of the press, as a gag, presented him with a slab of concrete with two solid foo   imbedded in it.

In anothe   ter he made it clear the decision had not been an easy one. "Next time I see you, I'll show you the nail holes in my hands," he wrote, adding, "I spent a few sleepless nights but as hard as we tried we could find no long-range solution other than this one. I still think the federal government perpetrated a crime on the people when it first spawned this, but the crime is almost a catching disease and, eventually, states like ours find no alternative."

A federal program that caused no end of problems for the Reagan administration was the Office of Economic Opportunity, also known as the War on Poverty, and especially one of its offspring, known as Rural Legal Assistance. The governor concluded that RLA lawyers were more interested in disrupting the orderly administration of the state for ideological reasons than they were in helping poor people with their legal problems.

Consequently, in January of 1971, as was his right under the law, he vetoed the OEO grant to RLA that would have allowed it to continue operating. A letter to Frank Carlucci, then director of OEO, tells what happened after that:

"Dear Mr. Carlucci:

"I am very much disturbed by recent actions of the federal Office of Economic Opportunity in relation to the investigation of the California Rural Legal Assistance program and by the treatment being afforded the California State Office of Economic Opportunity by federeal OEO.

"As you know, in January you made the determination that my veto of the CRLA grant should not be overridden.

Subsequently, you requested that we agree to a full investigation of CRLA by a commission and to a new short-term grant for a period of six months. We agreed to your requests on the basis that this would be helpful in determining how best to provide legal services to the rural poor in the areas that have been served by CRLA.

"Since that time the federal OEO has repeatedly breached the understandings which had been agreed to by you and other federal representatives and by representatives of my office and the state OEO. Members of your office have made false and misleading statements to the news media with respect to the firm understanding which was reached jointly by the State of California and the federal government. Further, the selection process and the orientation of the commission were not conducted in accordance with our understandings. This has resulted in the commission members being confused and misinformed as to the nature and procedures of their task, and has severely hindered them in carrying out their responsibilities.

"If testimony presented before the commission during the past week is true, there has also been a lack of objectivity and fairness within federal OEO in reviewing my veto of CRLA and the reasons supporting it. This has even included threats to hold up the granting of federal funds for other projects totally unrelated to CRLA, unless California altered its position.

"The actions by the federal OEO, which are clearly detrimental to the best interests of the citizens of California, apparently have been taken in an effort to curry favor with the Poverty Laws Establishment, and to appease certain ultraliberal members of Congress who consistently oppose the President on every issue.

"The most recent misconduct is the premature release to the news media of a report criticizing the state OEO, in violation of an agreement that such a report would not be made public until after California officials had had the opportunity to respond with corrections of numerous factual misstatements and erroneous conclusions contained in that report. This premature release, and the resulting adverse publicity, seem calculated to create a smoke screen to mask the revelation of federal OEO's improprieties in regard to the commission investigating CRLA, and to aid those who are seeking to abolish any effective controls or safeguarding of OEO funds and programs within our state.

"It is interesting to observe that our state OEO has been 'reviewed,' 'evaluated,' and 'audited' by the federal government four times in the past four months—commencing immediately after the governor's veto of the CRLA grant. We are informed that this recent attention is greater than that shown any other state, a fact that raises at least a suspicion of bureaucratic harassment.

"At all times in our dealings with federal OEO, the State of California has acted in good faith, believing that the agreements to which we were a party would be honored by you and your subordinates. We have been repeatedly disappointed to find that this has not been the case.

"I am requesting that you take immediate action to rectify this situation, to insure that further understandings with our officials will be honored and to prevent further instances of misconduct of the type outlined above. By separate letter to the President, I am requesting that a meeting be set up which will include you, representatives of my office, and your superiors, to establish necessary safeguards to govern the relationships between the federal OEO and the State of California so that these types of incidents will not occur again. It is essential that corrective action be taken so that we can act together for the best interests of all the citizens of California, including those whom the Economic Opportunity Act was intended to benefit."

The governor's letter to President Nixon read:

"Dear Mr. President:

"Since our visit in January, John Mitchell and his staff have been of great assistance to us in attempting to resolve the problems with the federal Office of Economic Opportunity. I am very grateful to you for your personal interest and to John for his assistance.

"During the past few months, however, numerous problems have continued to arise from within the federal OEO, as some of their personnel appear unwilling to carry out the decisions and understandings reached between the State of

California and the federal government. Enclosed is a copy of my letter to Frank Carlucci, which sets forth in detail these problems. Also enclosed is a copy of a letter that I was obliged to send to each member of the commission appointed to investigate the California Rural Legal Assistance program, to clarify our position and to advise them of the agreements made between federal OEO and my office.

"This situation has reached a point where the actions of federal OEO seriously jeopardize the ability of our state government to properly carry out its responsibilities under the Economic Opportunity Act and to assure our citizens that public funds are being properly used by OEO-funded agencies for the benefit of the poor. Therefore, I would appreciate your help in arranging a meeting which would include Frank Carlucci, representatives of my office, and such members of your staff as you may deem appropriate, so that we may resolve these problems and establish necessary safeguards to govern the relationships between federal OEO and the State of California. Such a meeting might be helpful to Mr. Carlucci because I am inclined to believe that sometimes members of his staff do not say to him the same things they say to us—or at least they shade it a bit. . . ."

One Washington proposal opposed by the Reagan administration was the Family Assistance Program of welfare reform advocated by the Nixon administration. Though the governor was never publicly critical of President Nixon, he felt that as a matter of principle he must oppose the Family Assistance Program. A letter to the president in 1970 sets forth the governor's misgivings:

"Dear Mr. President:

"My attempts to reach you on Monday and Tuesday having failed, I spoke with John Ehrlichman last evening. He felt that Mr. Nathan, of the Bureau of the Budget, might help answer some of the serious questions, concerns, and reservations we have regarding the Welfare Reform Act, as it came out of the House, and is now being considered by the Senate.

"Mr. Nathan consulted with my staff at length. However,

our general objections and reservations were outside his scope of authority. Additionally, while he expressed agreement with some of our objections, and even shared our concerns with one or two aspects, we received no assurance of what, if anything, the administration intends to do to amend the act accordingly.

"Meanwhile, I have today received a telegram from Chairman Long requesting my views on the proposed act. I intend to answer him fully and completely. I have been contacted by other governors and expect to have further conversations with them. In fairness to you and your administration, I hasten to send you herewith the essence of those reservations.

"In our meeting at San Clemente last August 13 when my staff and I had the opportunity to discuss welfare reform with you, we were elated at the proposals you outlined and, as I recall, offered to serve as a test state for the contemplated work-incentive part of the program you outlined.

"Since then, we have followed the progress of your program with a great deal of anticipation and, lately, apprehension. The evolution of the Welfare Reform Act—from your original message to the Congress on August 11, 1969, through Representative Byrnes' bill, to the Ways and Means Committee bill (HR 16311) as amended and passed by the House last week—has caused me increasing concern. Possibly you share my concern.

"My reservations about the Welfare Reform Act stem from a deep philosophical antipathy toward a government-guaranteed income and increasing federal intervention into state operations, and also my conviction that the bill will not accomplish your purposes as set forth in your August message to Congress. In addition, I have a real apprehension that the costs of the act will be excessive at a time when the taxpayer is already struggling to make ends meet.

"Let me set forth some of my specific concerns:

Work Incentive—
In your August message, you said, 'I propose that we make available an addition to the incomes of the "working poor" to encourage them to go on working

and to eliminate the possibility of making more from welfare than from wages.'

It seems to me that the act as passed by the House does *not* eliminate the possibility of making more from welfare than wages. It would be entirely possible for a family in which the father is fully employed to have less income than a family in which the father is working only part-time—and only slightly more income than if the father were not working at all. If you wish, we can supply specific data to support this statement.

Further, the act would encourage many now working their way off of the welfare rolls to fall back into a state of federal dependency.

Family Solidarity—

In your message to Congress, you said, 'The new plan rejects a policy that undermines family life. It would end the substantial financial incentives to desertion.' This is an objective which I support wholeheartedly.

But, under the Welfare Reform Bill as amended and passed by the House, very substantial incentives for desertion would remain. The bill could actually weaken incentives to maintain traditional family relationships and in some cases, may encourage dissolution of families.

Costs—

The act, as it came out of the House, appears to have all the earmarks of the open-ended welfare programs of the 60s—such as Medicare and Medicaid—whose costs have escalated beyond even the wildest sums predicted by their original opponents. Some of our staff predict—as do others in both the public and private sector—that the costs of this act could run as high as $15 billion.

I am convinced that, unless the Welfare Reform Act provides for funding solely from a specific surtax or dedicated tax, the taxpayers will be unaware of the extent of the real costs of the program and these costs will soon outpace any benefits which might be derived.

Government Income—
Although proponements of the new act claim it does not provide a government-guaranteed income, under this bill, no work-qualified head of household need actually work. He, or she, is simply required to state a need and *agree* to work or train to work to receive benefits. This is—in fact—a guaranteed income. I must oppose such a proposal.

Federal Controls—
In order to advance your concept of 'New Federalism,' those states which are able and which desire to administer the program themselves should be paid rather than penalized for performing services for a federal program. Those states which are unable to administer their own programs, or do not desire to do so, should be charged—*not* rewarded—for having the federal government perform the services for them.

The disincentives in the act encourage states to surrender their administrative operations to Washington; this can hardly be compatible with your desire for a 'New Federalism.' The act delegates to the Department of Health, Education & Welfare, and Labor unprecedented administrative powers. This makes it impossible to assess how various provisions are to be applied, and what impact these will have on state operations now and in the future.

(It seems to me that one of the stultifying effects of the act will be to impede, in some cases destroy, the growing and creative work-program efforts being put forth by the private sector. This will stifle ingenuity and freeze failure; and, this is completely out of phase with emerging programs to solve these welfare problems at the local level. It is of deep concern that there are no provisions permitting the states to engage in, or continue, pilot projects which might prove more responsive to state or local needs.)

In order to support healthier relationships between the federal and state governments—and your efforts to limit the expansion of bureaucracy—the act should be amended to prohibit the formation of any new administrative organization except that which is necessary to audit and reimburse those states which administer their own programs, and to provide administrative services for those states which do not. This latter organization should be only as large as can be funded by the charges collected from those states which are serviced.

"In summary, Mr. President, your original proposal sought to reduce the welfare rolls; the bill passed by the House does not even mention this as a goal or purpose. It will add fifteen million persons to the system, with no significant reduction in sight, based on HEW estimates of continually rising costs.

"Your stated goal was to reduce welfare costs (also not mentioned in the new act); this program will cost additional billions, based on HEW estimates.

"Your message to Congress specifically rejected the concept of a guaranteed income; the new bill provides every family with an income floor.

"You called for manpower programs to get individuals off of welfare and on to payrolls; yet many, if not most, of the 'working poor' to be added to the rolls under the House-amended bill live in rural areas where there are no training facilities and where there are, in fact, no jobs to train for.

"I'm sure you know how painful it is to find myself in the position of opposing this measure. Only the strongest convictions could bring me to this, but after struggling with the ever-growing problems of welfare these past few years, I'm convinced this is the greatest single domestic problem facing the nation.

"It may be that working in concert we can remove the

evils and correct the weaknesses of the House-passed bill and I offer my assistance."

Incidentally, although the president continued to support the proposed welfare program, it did not pass the Congress. It is generally agreed that the governor's adamant and carefully reasoned opposition was the main reason for its eventual failure.

One thing Governor Reagan has never been able to understand is the occasional accusations or innuendoes that he, or his administration or the Republican party are anti-Black or at least unfeeling in their attitudes toward them.

Very early in his first campaign for governor he stalked out of an all-Black Republican m⸺⸺because he felt two other gubernatorial candidates on the platform with him were implying that he was a racist.

He later went back to the meeting and cleared up any misunderstandings about why he had left.

One of his first acts upon becoming governor was to set up a minorities office within the governor's office, headed initially by a Mexican-American but for more than seven years by a Black. The office had ten field men scattered about the state, working within the minority communities and reporting back on minority problems to him or his executive assistant.

In 1968 Reagan held meetings throughout California with minority groups, both Hispanic and Black. Those were times of strong black militancy and some of the meetings were tense, to say the least.

In fact, the day the Washington, D. C., riots broke out immediately following the assassination of Dr. Martin Luther King, Governor Reagan was in Washington meeting with Black militants in the largely Black Southeast section of the city. He and his staffers barely made it back to his hotel, walking the last few blocks because whites fleeing the city so jammed the traffic his car could not move.

Despite his efforts to understand and deal with minority problems and even though he appointed more Blacks to high-level policy positions than any previous governor, Governor Reagan has always had to deal with the charge that he hasn't done enough.

A friendly letter from \ *h Cooley of Monroe, Louisi-
ana, in March 1978, mentic \ d that "you are 'short' in this
area" of working with Black. He replied that he recognizes
the problem and blamed it on "the image-making that goes
on today."

"I appointed more Blacks to executive and policy-making
positions than all the previous governors of California put
together. I am trying to contact Black leaders and correct
their misconception of me," he wrote.

When Ronald Reagan first became governor, he and Mrs.
Reagan were aghast at the mansion the state provided its
governor. A wooden Victorian building, it had once been
a boarding house. From its looks it might have housed the
Adams family. But, because of its downtown location and
the fact that it was a firetrap, it was not satisfactory for a
governor with growing children.

Because of this the Reagans moved into a private residence in East Sacramento. When his landlord threatened
to sell the house from under him, a group which included
some friends of the Reagans joined together to buy the
house and then rented it back to the governor.

This occasioned a humorous letter from the governor to
"Dear Landlord," which went to each of the group.

"Knowing you receive unjustified complaints and un-
deserved criticism from miserable and unhappy tenants, and
having a peculiar sympathy for anyone subject to that kind
of treatment, I thought you might enjoy hearing from a
happy tenant for a change.

"My wife and I are very glad you bought out our previous
landlord. (He should lose the money on the way to the
bank.) Somehow, the place looks brighter already, possibly
because we painted a little here and there. (We won't knock
out any walls, however, without letting you know.)

"Anyway, the hot water is hot when it should be; the
neighbors are quiet. (If they complain, they'll get a freeway
right through their piazza.) The fuses don't blow, even with
all the lights on, and it's only ten minutes to my job.

"Just changing landlords has my wife so revved up she
is pushing furniture all over the place (frankly, it gives me

a pain in the back); but we want you to know we love you, we thank you, and if keeping the place real nice will help show our appreciation, we'll do it. We don't even let the dog in the house, and the kids are severely limited."

The governor penned a jesting P.S.: "I am talking to the people I work for about lowering your taxes."

Almost from the beginning, the governor hoped to persuade the legislature to approve construction of a mansion that would be adequate for future governors. But partisan bickering more than any one thing prevented construction getting under way until late in the governor's second term.

He and Nancy were destined never to live in a governor's mansion worthy of California, but future governors will thanks to his efforts.

Letters to two legislators who opposed construction of the mansion on a river-bluff site about fifteen miles from the capitol tell of Governor Reagan's reasons for wanting it built.

To Robert Moretti, Democratic speaker of the Assembly, he wrote: "For almost forty years there seems to have been general agreement in Sacramento and elsewhere that California should have a new and suitable governor's residence. And yet for almost forty years such a project has foundered for the most part on the rocks of partisanship and bickering over fairly unimportant differences. I would hate to see that happen again.

"Right now the issue of location has been raised and with it some misstatements as to how the present site was chosen. Being the only person at hand with personal experience in holding this job and living for a time in a downtown location, subsequently in a residential neighborhood, I'd like to offer some thoughts based on that experience.

"First of all, in this position it is difficult enough to maintain a normal family life and to raise children without making them live and grow up in a public edifice. I'm quite sure future governors are going to have school-age children. If the governor's residence is going to be downtown, a part of the capitol complex, who do they play with when they come home from school? I can attest to the fact that living in a downtown location they don't run out the back door

and across the street or down the block to join schoolmates
or neighborhood friends. This problem would be vastly
multiplied if the original concept were followed of making
the residence also house the executive offices. That's a great
escape from the grist mill—taking an elevator from the
office to an upstairs apartment. Believe me, a residence that
is a home, and not an office complex, located in a residential
neighborhood is a necessity."

In this letter Governor Reagan referred to the spurious
contention that the proposed location was of archaeological
value because it had been the site of either an Indian village
or Indian burial ground or both. Some anti-Reagan Indians
also used this issue as a reason to oppose the mansion. T'
were aided in that effort by the then secretary of state and
present governor, Edmund G. Brown, Jr. Brown, a bach-
elor, on assuming office attempted in vain to stop construction of the mansion. For reasons unclear he has declared
he will never live in it. Governor Reagan, however, believes
future governors will.

In his letter to Moretti the governor discussed the Indian
Village objection and ended with a plea for Moretti's cooperation:

"Since then the legislature has approved the site, appro-
priated the necessary funds, and an architectural firm has
been selected in the manner prescribed by law. As for the
possibility of the site being the locale of an ancient Indian
village—this will only be known if an archaeological dig
verifies it. If so, you have passed and I have signed a bill
ordering that any remains be reinterred on the land in an
area that will not be covered by structures. I would think
that a plot could be set aside, properly marked and cared
for. Incidentally, since archaeologists have declared that if
such a village once existed there it was 3,000 years ago,
I don't believe anyone alive today can claim relationship
to those who lived in the village.

"Whatever our political differences, can't we go forward
on this and at long last give California an official residence
for its governors in a location that is as beautiful as anything
the Sacramento area has to offer? This can be something

of which all of us can be proud and for which future governors will be grateful."

In a letter to Assemblyman John Vasconcellos, also a Democrat, Reagan asked him to "reconsider your position," and pointed out that, "My predecessor, Governor Brown, and Mrs. Brown feel there should be a new residence and indeed were victims themselves of the political controversy that arose when they tried to bring this about. They've expressed their belief in the need after eight years' experience in the job. Governors before them have been of like mind. Is there some significance to the fact that several governors of widely divergent views have been in agreement on this subject even when they no longer were personally affected?

"I think it would be a tragedy to relinquish the building site which has been given to the state, waste hundreds of thousands of dollars by halting construction and extend the forty years of political wrangling."

All of Governor Reagan's political letters were not to fellow office-holders or politicians. Neither did all of them deal with subjects as all-encompassing as tax or welfare reform or as personal as the mansion.

In one letter he opposed efforts to give California a unicameral (one-house) legislature. "There is much to be said for the check and balance and the added deliberative process in having two houses," he wrote. He believes that compromises worked out in conferences between two legislative houses are "good for the people in the long run."

In a letter to a "frustrated" constituent he explained a tax reduction and limitation program that eventually was to be submitted to the people in a special election. Known familiarly as "Prop. One," the proposal lost because, the governor was firmly convinced, people believed dishonest opposition charges that it was really a tax-shift program. It was, perhaps, the only time the governor was unable to sell a program of his directly to the people of California. Here is his explanation of the proposal:

"When I say I share your frustration, let me point out the reason. No administration has worked harder at cutting the cost of individual programs and no administration has been more successful in reducing the cost of those programs. Yet, government continues to grow at every level in size and in cost. This is why we had a task force appointed over a year ago to see if there was some other way that government spending could be held down. They came in with this proposal for a fifteen-year plan of gradually reducing the percentage of your income the state could take without your permission, and then putting a limitation about 20 percent less than the present level at the end of that period, in the Constitution so that only by your vote—by a vote of the people—could government ever go beyond that limit. In addition, we added to this the rebate of 20 percent of this year's income tax and a proposal to reduce permanently the income tax by 7½ percent. Individuals with a taxable income of below $4,000 and families earning less than $8,∂∧∖ will have no state tax-liability at all.

"I urge you to support this measure because it is probably the last chance to ever put a limitation on government spending. It can set the stage for a new approach in other states and even at the national level."

In the same letter he answered a number of other complaints from the frustrated constituent: "Now, as to your disillusionment with the party and the desired change, may I just remind you of a few facts, hopefully to set the record straight. What would the budget be if in addition to the Democratic majority in the legislature, there had been a Democratic governor with the same philosophy? I have vetoed out of the budget over these six years more than a billion dollars in increased spending that had been added in by the legislature after I sent the budget upstairs. The budget would be a billion dollars larger than it is had these vetoes not taken place. The only year since I have been governor that I did not have to veto any money out of the budget was the one year we had a Republican majority in the legislature. In that year the budget came down as I sent it upstairs, with no additional spending. In last year's budget alone I vetoed $503 million out. Now, in addition to this, I have vetoed appropriations and spending bills introduced throughout the regular legislative session. I have no total on those but it could well exceed another billion dollars.

Last year I vetoed 168 measures. In every instance, the Democratic majority tried to override my veto but our Republican legislators held firm and our opponents could not get the two-thirds majority necessary.

"With regard to state-employee salary increases let me call your attention to what is mandated by law. The law says these employees must be paid comparable to salaries in the private sector for people doing comparable work. Three years ago we held our employees at no salary increase at all. Now, complying with the law and over a three-year period, we are making adjustments to bring them up to the level of the private sector.

"I agree with you that Watergate has had a very depressing effect upon our country. I don't think, however, it is fair to conclude that there are no dedicated people in government. Actually, the people in government are pretty much the same as in any group. They are no better or no worse than the people who send them there.

"If I may make one last point. You speak of politicians. I never in my entire life had any desire to run for public office. I was finally persuaded to do this by a group of people who shared my beliefs. I felt as you do that something had to be done. I gave up a career that was rewarding me at a rate of five times my present salary in government. I don't think of myself as a politician. I think of myself as a citizen who took this chore on to try to accomplish something."

Writing to the Reverend David R. Ellingson in 1974, Governor Reagan touched on the dangers of high costs of government. "I am convinced that this country must take the lead in controlling the cost of government which leads to inflation, and, thus stop this runaway increase in prices as well as the enormous tax burden being borne by the people. Until we do, we are going to see our standard of living for the great middle class of America continuing to decline. The worst part of all this is that not only does the standard of living decline, but we are saddling future generations with an unbearable debt because of our continued deficit funding."

Another problem that beset the Reagan administration

in its early years was the very emotional issue of mental illness, and how much money the state should spend in caring for the mentally ill and the mentally retarded. This was another area in which reporters and people who were emotionally—or politically—involved ignored what the governor was attempting to do and attacked him as a man who put money ahead of humanitarian concepts and who was heartless and cruel.

In his continuing effort to keep the record straight, Governor Reagan as late as 1974 wrote to one father; ". . . I wanted to clear the air regarding some misunderstandings about our mental health-care policy and the possibility of hospital closings.

"In spite of what some hospital employees might say, there has been no economy move at the expense of the mentally ill. The program of transferring many patients from state hospitals to county mental health-care clinics is dictated by legislation passed several years ago before I became governor. Actually, our budget, staffing, and our per-patient cost has gone up considerably, and we do not regret this. The legislation I refer to was based on the professionals' belief that smaller, more localized treatment centers and hospitals could do a better job than the large state institutions which in too many instances had simply become warehouses providing only custodial care.

"The hospital population at the beginning of the bill was some 37,000. By the time I became governor it was 26,000. It has now been reduced to less than 10,000. In no instance, however, was anyone forced out of the hospital. They could only be removed when counties notified us they had the facilities and were now prepared to take over their citizens who were in the state hospitals. These county clinics, under the previous administration, were subsidized between 50 and 75 percent of the cost. We are subsidizing them at 90 percent of the cost. I will admit that we did find instances where counties were over-optimistic, and in their desire to get operations underway, asked for patients when they actually did not have all the facilities required. We have taken, and are taking, steps to change this to make sure the counties can handle the cases properly.

"Naturally, as the hospital population declined, there were some closings and consolidations. Perhaps in the future there will be more. There is, however, no intention of totally eliminating the state hospital. We realize not only the need for research but principally the need for custodial care for those who cannot be helped by the smaller county clinics. We have done our best to make the employees in the state hospital understand the long-range plans and that there is no immediate threat to these hospitals or to their positions. In spite of this, the rumor mill grinds and the morale persists. I have to say that some of this, I feel, is engendered by employees who have never believed in the legislation changing the policy and are trying to retain the original concept of the large warehouse-type hospital.

"In all of this, I know there are instances, and perhaps you are the victim of one of these, where certain hospitals or even certain wards within hospitals are not up to the standard we have tried to maintain. Sometimes this is a temporary situation due to an inability to hire and fill positions. Sometimes it's just slack administration."

The decline in numbers of mental-hospital patients early in the Reagan administration brought a corresponding cut in hospital staffing. Ignoring the fact that staff-to-patient ratios remained *higher* than in any major state, opponents of the governor accused him of cutting back on care for the mentally ill in order to save money. Despite all efforts to explain the program to the public, some of the resentment against Ronald Reagan, fostered by this false charge, lingered throughout his entire eight years as governor.

The question of how elected public servants should be paid was another that brought a letter from Governor Reagan to a constituent: "I confess I don't have a totally satisfactory answer, but lean very much toward the idea of salary and allowances, which make it possible for a dedicated individual to serve even though he has no personal wealth. If we want a man's best thinking applied to our community problems, we should see that he is reasonably sure of being able to provide for his family and the education of his children."

The governor also suggested that it would be of value

to have a study measuring whether "a George Meany rate[s] a salary . . . nearly double that of a United States senator" or whether a state university president should make more than the governor of that state. It happens that in California the president of the university system is paid more than the governor.

Another letter voicing a constituent's laundry list of complaints brought the reply that "I have been sitting here puzzling over how I can answer your letter without sounding like a politician making promises."

He then continued: "You spoke of unkept promises about reform of welfare and some of the other things that are wrong in government. May I just point out that many of us who are supposedly making the promises are most sincere and are trying to achieve the reforms. But we are frustrated because vested interest groups, such as the Welfare Rights Organization, the Welfare Workers Union, and numerous groups created by OEO grants, have become powerful lobbying forces able to launch widespread propaganda and able to sway votes to keep reform efforts bottled up in legislative committees or rejected in the final vote on the floor.

"I believe very deeply in the so-called 'silent majority,' the people like yourself who make this country run, who send the kids to school, pay the bills, pay the taxes, and only now and then raise a voice as you have in legitimate protest. Further, I have tried to keep myself in the position of representing that 'silent majority,' as obligated to stand between the taxpayers and the tax-spenders. I am not alone in government. There are many more who share that idea, but we very much need the help of people like you. We need voices on our side when we take stands against spending on behalf of the taxpayer because, heaven only knows, the capitol can fill up very fast with the voices from those other groups.

"I have told this legislature we have reached a time for choosing. We can meet our fiscal problems in government by adding to your burden with more taxes, or we can have the guts to cut back the size and cost of this government and reform welfare and stop giving money to people who are not truly dependent on the rest of us. I choose this latter course.

"In these next few months you are going to see a very bloody battle here in our capitol. I wish I could reply to your letter with some assurance that automatically and immediately things are going to be better. I can only say, don't give up just yet. You are not alone and there is going to be a fight. And your help will be needed."

Agricultural problems also came to the governor's attention. In more than one case he had to disappoint his friends in this great California industry. For instance, California's peach growers, generally strong supporters of the governor, wanted him to sign a bill that would have limited and controlled the planting of cling-peach orchards.

Governor Reagan vetoed the bill and wrote to Ralph B. Bunje, general manager of the California Canning Peach Association, that "seldom has a bill caused me so much mental anguish as this one.

"I am well aware of the hardships and the problems affecting the peach growers, and as you know I have ordered Earl Coke and Jerry Fielder to bend every effort to see if they cannot find ways to help in this situation. I found, however, I could not in clear conscience sign the bill which arrived on my desk. It was contrary to everything I think is our philosophy, and not a valid answer to the present problem. Over the long run, the precedent it established ld, in my opinion, be destructive of the very system we are trying to defend. It literally said that those now engaged in the business could, by their vote, keep anyone else from ever coming in. Growers from a half-dozen different crops were lined waiting with similar legislation. Believe me, I tried to find some reason within the bill which would permit me to sign it, and could not."

Turning down friends and then explaining "why" to them is one of the more uncomfortable duties a governor has. When old-time actor-singer Pinky Tomlin, a staunch Republican, called, recommending a friend for a judgeship, the governor replied by letter: "Confirming our recent phone conversations, I have to say with great regret that while your friend is qualified regarding a judicial appointment, there just seems to be in that particular area a great wealth of talent. Under the system we've been using of screening all possibilities through a variety of committees—local bar, local laymen, state bar and so forth—a number do come out ahead in the ratings.

"For all these four years, I've tried very hard to abide by this rating system so that those doing the ratings would realize not only did they have a responsibility, but that their careful screening was the basis upon which appointments were made. For that reason, I just can't skip down and make an appointment which would be obviously bypassing some of their choices.

"I know how much this means to you, and I'm sure your friend must be aware of all that you've done in his behalf. Let me just say we will of course keep his name here on tap in the event that any changes may occur. But again, I must say realistically, there are so many in this particular area that I can't hold out too much hope. I know you'll understand. Again my regrets."

No book about Governor Reagan would be complete without the mention of jelly beans. The governor and the jelly bean arrived in Sacramento simultaneously and they soon became a trademark of his office.

There were some misconceptions about them, as there always is when people begin trying to trace the growth of a tradition without going to its source.

This letter to Dr. Alcides Pinto, director of research at the Crownsville, Maryland, State Hospital, sets the record straight in the governor's own words.

"I'm afraid a certain amount of distortion has resulted from the distance the story has traveled. Apparently a somewhat humorous incident has been portrayed as a system for breaking the smoking habit. Unfortunately, I have no such system.

"Some years ago when I gave up smoking I found the most trying times were those periods immediately after lunch and dinner—especially dinner. I began popping a few jelly beans in my mouth and that in itself became a habit.

"A friend delivered a large jar of jelly beans to me here in the capitol my first day in office. It was quite a joke for awhile, since I left the jar on the Cabinet Room table. Evidently no one really ever outgrows the childhood love for jelly beans. The jar has been refilled many times over these six years and our cabinet meetings go on with the jar being passed around during even the most solemn of meetings. Cabinet and staff have become jelly-bean users. There isn't a great deal of smoking in the meetings, but I don't know whether this can be credited to the candy.

"I'm sorry if the news stories have raised any false hopes."

In another letter, referring to "the place jelly beans have in this administration," the governor wrote, "some political figures have en⌐⌐⌐d in history as lions or conquerors or something e⌐ ⌐⌐ly impressive. It's a little frightening to think California history might record us as jelly beans."

Rib ticklers usually drew responses from Governor Reagan who loves a funny story, a one-liner, or a quip, although he groans at puns.

W. E. Bolton of Castro Valley wrote the following letter to the governor.

"Governor, I may never smile again!

"I am a man, you see, and I feel I have been cheated. I've been listening to some women on television hold forth on this new fad called Women's Liberation and I developed a great feeling of emptiness in my chest. Women need to be liberated like a humming bird needs a flight manual.

"What I am saying isn't against women. Not in the least. I love women. They are good conversational companions; they bring light into a man's life.

"But I sneer at their current drive for liberation—whatever the hell that means.

"I know where women come from. God made the first one, Eve, from one of Adam's ribs . . . and I think that was where all the trouble started. It all boils down to simple jealousy!

"Women are jealous of men!

"But the peculiar thing is that men really should be jealous of women. Think about it. Who was the ugliest person you ever knew? Some man, right? And the prettiest? A woman, of course. Who gets all the proposals—not to mention the propositions. Women are first! Yes they are. What's the president's wife called? The First Lady. Did you ever hear of some famous woman's husband being saluted as the First Man? No. Only Adam has that honor.

"Some honor.

"Who let himself be carved up so Eve could be fabricated? Do you think for one minute she would have given up one of her bones to create man? A fingernail maybe, but God would have had a second hell on his hands if He'd asked a woman to part with anything substantial just to make a bedfellow.

"You know when I was just a boy growing up in the Bible Belt, it was an accepted fact that women have one more rib than does man.

"Of course they were wrong.

"There are two more in the female.

"Figure it out, she has all of hers, plus one of his; he has one less than all of his. Or, she has her full q~ ~ ~lus one, while he has his full quota, minus one. Get it?

"Now what in hell is a poor rib-deprived man supposed to do?

"Governor, please give it some thought. Privately, I doubt that we will ever be able to get our rib back after all this time. But don't you agree that we ought to get something out of the deal?"

Governor Reagan responded:

"I have read your letter anent ribs and women with great interest.

"I am pleased to tell you I share your views about women's liberation. At the same time, I have to say I'm greatly pleased with the twenty-three ribs that have been assigned to me under the marital customs of our society. While I feel no need personally for the proposal you make to restore equity in the matter of the missing rib, I have asked my legal advisers to look into all the ramifications of such a change in the law.

"However, and above all, I want to thank you from the bottom of my heart for your letter. Your complaint about the missing rib is the only thing I haven't been blamed for since I've been in this damn job."

As the days of his administration dwindled the governor began receiving letters praising him for his outstanding record as governor. Because this is a book primarily of letters *from* the governor, I must omit most of them, but nevertheless two or three, I think, are appropriate.

One, from Democratic assemblyman Wadie P. Deddeh, said in part: ". . . I have deemed it an honor and a privilege to work with you these past years.

"You have manifested a sincerity of purpose, an enormous amount of personal energy, a real dedication and a sense of philosophy which elevates political discussion to the high level of philosophy. . . .

"You and Mrs. Reagan, not unlike other good and past first families of our state, have consistently set for us an example of personal integrity and maturity of individual behavior that cannot be lost, as a lesson for our young people. . . .

". . . as you retire from the governorship, I would hope you will continue to be a voice of high philosophical character in the public dialogue of the coming years."

The governor, obviously touched, responded: "Your letter has to be one of the nicest things that's happened to me in these almost eight years. I thank you from the bottom of my heart."

Another unexpected letter came from a state-university administrator. "Well," began the letter, "I guess I need to say that, in my judgment and after eight years of your administration, you've been a damn good governor.

"There is of course the fiction that you've destroyed either the University of California or the California State University and Colleges, or both, but you know and I know—and every thoughtful, analytic person knows—that is not true. Indeed, in my judgment, while you might have been from time to time too tight on the reins your overall support for higher education, and especially the CSUC, has been adequate and beneficial.

"But your contribution has been in another direction, really: forcing us in higher education to reexamine our beliefs, our values, our directions, our policies, and procedures. In a certain sense your very early 'cut, squeeze, and trim' proposal (remember the 10 percent across-the-board cutback in early 1967?) got our attention in the same way the mule-master gets the attention of the mule—you sure got my attention, and in the last seven years I've come to see that a great deal, most if not all, of what you were trying to say to my colleagues and me surely makes sense, academically and fiscally.

"My 'conversion' started, but did not finish, during the year . . . of greatest activism: the moratoria, the Cambodian incursion, and the actual use of violence. I think, until that year, I really didn't believe in my heart that faculty members could be so irresponsible, that their 'liberal principles' were so damn flexible as not to be principles but mere prejudices and whims. I learned; and you do not know it, but you helped teach me—you went to most [of] the CSUC board meetings then, and spoke, and I tried to listen and understand. Finally, I did.

"Hence this letter, which is an awkward attempt to express a kind of belated appreciation. You've been a good governor, and equally important, a good educator in the lessons you've taught. I only wish it were you, and not the governor-elect, who'd occupy your office for the next four years."

In his reply the governor said, "I'll take many memories and a few mementos with me, and your letter will be one of those. You've made me very proud and truly grateful."

Caspar W. Weinberger, HEW secretary when the governor's second term ended but earlier Reagan's finance director, also wrote. He noted reading "many fine tributes" but added that "none of them I think quite caught the achievement which I thought was the greatest, and that was that almost single-handedly you turned around a great deal of thinking about government and the role of the State, and had more to do with the necessary changing attitudes than anyone in recent times."

Reagan responded that "this certainly is a time for mixed emotions. In one way, I miss the challenge and the opportunity to deal directly with the problems." Then he added that out of office he has "a sense of freedom that I didn't realize I had lost until I found it again."

Another letter came from Ed Davis, then Los Angeles Chief of Police, who wrote, "You have saved us from an irresponsible legislature by vetoing dangerous legislation. Who is going to protect us now?" The letter continued that "Because of your excellent service, California is in a lot better shape than it would be otherwise."

"I share your concern about the present legislature and certainly will do all I can to arouse public opinion if they head in the direction I suspect they will," Reagan promised in a return letter.

Finally, there is a last bit of correspondence between Ronald Reagan and S. I. Hayakawa, now a United States senator, but then president of the State University in San Francisco. Hayakawa's letter is signed in Japanese, "Your favorite Samurai." Here are the letters:

"Dear Dutch:

"I want you to know, as you leave office, that it was a pleasure and an honor to have been a state college president during your administration. I want to thank you for the abundant moral and practical support you gave me, both before the general public and before the trustees of the state college system.

"Some of my academic colleagues foolishly regard you as an enemy of higher education because you insisted on professional responsibility in the faculty and civility among students.

"I want you to know that a majority of us, both professors and administrators, believe that you have been a good friend of education. Both the California State University and Colleges system and the University of California system have come a long way since the dreadful days of 1968, '69 and '70. You have helped enormously in bringing about this change.

"Every good wish to you in your future undertakings, whatever they may be.

"Sincerely yours,

   "(Translation: Your favorite Samurai.)"

"Dear Samurai:

   "Your letter is more appreciated than words can tell and it shall be kept with those very special things I take with me when I leave. Indeed, it is my only letter from a campus president in either of the two systems.

   "It seems a long way back to those dark days when you breached the barricade. Yet in some ways it seems only yesterday. I believe it marked a turning point in the insanity that gripped so much of academia, and you were very much responsible for the turning.

   "Again, I thank you and I hope our paths will cross often in the days ahead."

The Citizen-Politician

I CONSIDER MYSELF very fortunate. In a time when many
Americans have become cynics about their government and
their elected representatives, I feel confident and ever more
devoted to our system. Why? Because I have had an opportunity to observe firsthand how it works and who makes
it run.

Granted, not all aspects of politics are appealing. Campaigns and an all-encompassing desire to win on the part
of those participants can bring out the worst in people. And
there are those public servants who take advantage of their
positions, don't do their homework, and base their actions
solely on the votes they may bring.

I do not say it is wrong for officeholders to listen to the
people. It is essential that those in government do listen.
However, there is a greater duty. If, as an elected official,
you gain information that suggests that many people are
wrong or misguided in their support of or opposition to an
issue, you have a responsibility to inform them and to act
in their best interest, as you see it, regardless of the consequences. It's always disheartening to see a greater number
of legislators than I would like to admit take the easy way,
instead of the principled way, in order to assure their re-
election. But then there are statesmen, like Ronald Reagan,

who are as forthright champions of the people and their own principles as you could ever find.

I know that the answer to the problems of our state and nation is to find and elect better candidates, not to change the system that has served us well for nearly 200 years.

Being a politician doesn't always make one an object of unqualified admiration. Ronald Reagan knew this before he ever sought office. Hence his description of himself while running for governor for the first time, as a "citizen-politician." But to some people a politician is a politician is a politician. And that viewpoint brought a reply to a letter from Mrs. Marjorie P. Gallion of Crane, Texas.

"I take exception," the governor wrote, "to one line in your October 20 letter. That is that I am a politician and therefore undeserving of your unqs... d support."

Then he explained: ". . . I came to this job never having sought it, never having believed that I should be in public office, and believing only that a set of circumstances had placed me here as a citizen with an opportunity to do something in behalf of the philosophy and the ideas which I supported. I have repeatedly told my cabinet and staff that we belong here only so long as we refer to government as 'they,' and never think of government as 'we.' I made a pledge to myself that I would make every decision on the basis that I would never run for office again. I didn't mean that I wouldn't run, but I felt that the first time a man in public office makes a decision on the basis of what it might or might not do with regard to votes in the next election, he has begun the path of compromise from which there is no turning back. I have kept that pledge."

The letter, written in 1971, was one of a number of pre-Watergate letters in which he strongly defended President Nixon. He wrote: "All I tried to indicate to you in my last letter was that the president had to deal with things as they are, not as he would like them to be. Bluntly, he inherited a situation in which the Democratic leadership had allowed the strength of this nation to deteriorate until we are in a situation where the possibility exists of the Soviet Union delivering an ultimatum. Since the president is the only man with access to all the information and all the facts necessary for a decision, I believe we must permit him to make those decisions, making sure, of course, that he is aware of the basic feelings of our people. It is my opinion that President Nixon has not shown that he goes along with the appeasement policy of the previous administrations. If I am wrong in this, I will be the first to repudiate him. Until such time, however, I believe we should go along with his decisions."

Time and again the governor explained in letters that "I gave up a career I loved—certainly an affluence I could never hope to match in public life—all at the very point when I could have both my career and the leisure to enjoy the hobby and sport (ranching) which I loved as much as my career."

"Does it . . . rational," he asked in one letter, "that I would make such a sacrifice and then for political expediency go against those convictions?

"When my present term is up, I've made it plain I'll not seek another. I've also made it plain I want no federal appointment. I intend to serve as governor, God willing, through these next three years.

"My beliefs now are the beliefs I held when I first ran for this office, when I campaigned for Barry Goldwater in '64, and for the years previous to that when, as a citizen, I traveled coast to coast speaking on behalf of conservative principles. Indeed, I chose to continue speaking even when to continue meant the loss of my television show."

Here, again, he was . . . ng to a person obviously disillusioned with President Nixon prior to Watergate. "Yes," he admitted, "there are things I might have chosen to do differently [from Nixon] but . . . I believe there is a better chance to advance my conservative principles with a Republican president, even though I disagree with some of what he does. I believe we have a better chance to elect a conservative president in 1976 if he doesn't have to run against an incumbent Democrat. I believe this country could very well cease to exist as a free nation if [a certain] one of the present Democrat challengers should be in charge for these next four years."

Governor Reagan always looked on Richard Nixon not

only as the president but also as a fellow Republican, as
a person of generally conservative political philosophy, and
as a friend.

As one American who greatly respects the office of the
presidency, the governor has been loath to attack any president, whether it was Truman, Eisenhower, Kennedy, Johnson, or Nixon. He has tried to keep his criticisms impersonal
and aimed at the issues, not at the person.

Because he campaigned strenuously for President Nixon's
election—and re-election—the governor felt a special obligation to give the president as much support as possible
as he attempted to solve our country's most pressing problems and, at the same time, put it on a more conservative
course.

As a friend the governor was always prepared to walk
the extra mile with President Nixon, which he did in the
case of Watergate, over the protests, I might add, of many
of his political advisers. Many of these advisers felt that
President Nixon had not returned the kind of friendship and
loyalty given him by the governor. Many felt, also, that
because of his strong defense of Nixon up until the day
Nixon admitted his early knowledge of the Watergate cover-
up, the stigma of the scandal would rub off on the governor
and hurt his political career.

People who have the governor's best interests at heart
sometimes forget that he always does what he thinks is the
right thing and the decent thing—remember, in an earlier
chapter where he talks about "always do and say the kindest
thing"—regardless of how much others think it might hurt
him.

I think one of the reasons Governor Reagan remained
popular with the people of California all during his eight
years in office is that he never forgot this and they instinc-
tively always knew it of him.

But though he has "done and said the kindest things"
about the former president it is plain to those who know
him that Governor Reagan was deeply hurt and disappointed
not only by Nixon's resignation but also by the actions and
statements that finally came to light and forced his resignation.

The few instances of wrongdoing or the appearance of wrongdoing in his own administration were dealt with swiftly and firmly by the governor. As a result, his was one of the most scandal-free administrations in California's history. It is difficult for him to understand why President Nixon was unable to do likewise.

In still another letter the governor protested that "I didn't want to be a candidate or an officeholder. I didn't seek it, indeed I fought against it and then gave up a pattern of living I had worked a long time for." But he went on to say that "I am not complaining—this has been the most soul-satisfying thing I've ever done, but only because I, too, believed in a principle and am realizing the joy of battling, yes, and sacrificing to implement that principle."

Here, too, he contrasted his continuing support of Nixon's philosophy and actions to those of the Democrats. "I do not believe he has departed from his basic Republican philosophy. Certainly there is deficit spending and controls, but there is also a near runaway inflation he inherited, plus the economic dislocation that comes from winding down a war. I happen to know that he considers the measures he felt he had to take as bitter medicine for a temporary illness. By contrast, our Democratic opponents would control the economy on a permanent basis and have expressed a belief in an ongoing program of deficit spending in good times as well as bad.

"Perhaps the China visit is viewed with alarm. But what do we know of the intricacies of a worldwide chess game in which we are no longer number one militarily? The eight years of Camelot and the Great Society wasted away our defenses to an extent far more dangerous than most of us appreciate. Isn't it possible that the president is playing for time and elbowroom, aware that two potential enemies are presently at odds with each other? Aren't we better off if Russia feels it has to keep those 140 divisions on the Chinese border?"

In 1971 and early 1972 conservative protests about President Nixon often took the form of asking the governor to run against him. He always refused. Here is a letter to Ron

Docksai, national chairman of the Young Americans for Freedom, that is typical of those refusals:

"Dear Mr. Docksai:

"I have just learned (from the press) of the plans Y.A.F. has for carrying on a presidential campaign in my behalf. While I am naturally proud that you hold me in such high regard, I still must ask with all the urgency I can express that you desist. To publicly repudiate any activity of Y.A.F. is not something I'm eager to do but, in this instance, I'll have no alternative if this effort continues.

"Let me presume on some seniority in the cause which has united us and plead with you to reconsider your position on Vietnam. It has been my privilege as a governor to receive in-depth briefings on the war and the international situation. As a result, I'm in full support of the president's Vietnamization policy.

"It is impossible to view Vietnam without taking into consideration where it fits into the gigantic chess game called the cold war. The stakes in that game are no less than our very existence, and only the president has access to all the facts necessary for each move.

"We've come a long way since those pre-Goldwater days when there were so very few of us sounding the alarm. We've elected a president, but he is opposed by a hostile Congress determined to deny almost every request he makes. The great permanent structure of government, the bureaucracy, resorts to outright sabotage as part of the effort to put back in power those who will renew the 'trip' this country was on for the eight New Frontier and Great Society years.

"The move you've announced can only divide and destroy our chance to go forward. I am pledged to support the president and have told him I'll lead a California delegation to the convention in his behalf. I ask you to join me in this lest we awaken to find those who oppose our dreams and goals returned to power. Ours is an uphill and long-term fight against a combination of mass media and political forces who deny everything in which we believe. We cannot afford division."

The governor, as a Republican, publically supported President Nixon whenever possible, and when he differed with him on an issue, as he freely but privately admitted he sometimes did, he refused to take his differences to the press. But that kind of loyalty, though it held conservatives in line and helped the president over many rough spots, was not, in my opinion, reciprocated by the president. Neither was it enough for some old-line Nixon supporters.

Many of these had never forgiven Reagan for making a run for the presidency in 1968 nor had some of them forgiven him for winning the 1966 California Republican gubernatorial primary. They had wanted one of their own, former San Francisco Mayor George Christopher, to be governor. The people of California, however, made the final decision.

Some political decisions, or rather decisions made about politics, can cause bitterness and unhappiness in old friends and political allies. One such case arose when the governor broke his own rule by supporting a candidate in a Republican primary. Another of the GOP candidates was, like the first, a Reagan friend and supporter. He wrote to him that "I'm sure you can tell from what I've been saying lately, I am deeply, deeply disappointed and hurt by the position of those who claim to lead my party and its office holders—often, like yourself, my friends as well—who have given their endorsement to [the other candidate] in his campaign against me."

The governor responded:

"I have received your letter and am terribly sorry about the situation in which we find ourselves. I have always been aware of your great service and loyalty to the party and have admired and respected you for it. I didn't know you were even considering this race, but let me explain my obligation to Newt, and I hope this will do something to indicate to your wife that I do try to return favors even if, in this instance, you seem to be the victim.

"Several years ago when we had just obtained a bare majority in the legislature and it looked as if we were, perhaps, going to be able to build on that and finally get out from under the years we've had here of bucking a

Democratic majority, Newt had a great opportunity, but it would have eliminated our one-point lead in the assembly. I'm speaking of the vacancy created in his congressional district. Newt was beseeched by all his friends to seek that office, and I don't think there is any question but that his election would have been automatic. He would today be a United States congressman. I asked him, on behalf of the party, to stay in the assembly and help us maintain the bare majority we had achieved. He did a lot of soul-searching and then came in one day and said out of loyalty to the party he would stay here and forego the opportunity for congress. I told him then he had an IOU that not only myself but the party owed him and owed him well. He never called on me for any kind of favor until John Harmer's appointment and then he said to me that now, once again, he wanted to make a run for something other than the assembly and this was it, John's senate seat.

"I didn't see how I could do anything but support him in view of the generous thing he had done several years ago and the promise I had made. You know how I have observed neutrality during all these years, but now I come down to my last two months in office, my last chance to repay a debt, an obligation which I made several years before and I feel I had no choice. As I said before, I had no way of anticipating that you might be interested in this race and for that I am sorry. I repeat you have been a loyal ally and I owe you a great debt of gratitude. I hope you can understand, however, that in this instance, I had a commitment I could not ignore."

Many of the governor's letters attempt to interpret the president's pre-Watergate actions to others. In a letter to an old friend, Ben T. Shaw, publisher of the *Dixon Evening Telegraph*, he wrote:

"I think the president has a consuming desire to resolve the international situation and, frankly, has little concern or interest in domestic problems. For this reason, I think he entrusted the domestic problems to people not in keeping with his philosophy. I know he has been misinformed as to some legislative proposals, such as supporting the welfare bill. Senator John Williams heard the briefing given to him by HEW and told a fellow senator that if he did not know what he knows about welfare he would have favored the bill on the basis of that briefing.

"I suppose that what I'm saying is that the president is still of a basic philosophy that has not changed. But he needs to involve himself more in the great domestic problems. Here, I believe, we can have an effect. I don't think we've done enough to call these matters to his attention, or to influence him in another direction. I also believe that he is becoming more aware of the need for more involvement in domestic affair

"Knowing the d   ̄ ̄e posture he inherited, plus t peace sentiment sweeping the country and the shaky fina cial situation, I believe he has done well on the foreig scene. He told me the other day directly in answer to m question that if Red China attempts to take back Taiwa by force this country will protect and defend Taiwan. He told me also with regard to the A   blast that even if the supreme court had ruled that he   ould not trigger the blast, he was going to go ahead and do it anyway regardless of the consequences, because it was so vital to our national defense.

"With this in mind and with the possibility of a Democratic victory, which we absolutely cannot afford, I have to say that I believe we should go forward in ensuring his re-election, but at the same time not be hesitant about exerting pressure to secure passage of more conservative policies. I think his recent veto of the Child-Care Bill which I had talked to him about is an indication of what I said a few lines back about his growing awareness of the importance of his domestic decisions. There certainly is nothing wrong with you pressuring him editorial-wise toward more conservative decisions, but my hope would be that you would do this as a supporter urging a course of action rather than giving the impression of one who has chosen a different course."

In a letter to M. Stanton Evans, head of the American Conservative Union, the governor discussed Nixon's visit to Red China, a visit that upset many conservatives.

"Stan, let me suggest something about the China visit

that, unfortunately, the president can't say, or for that matter, I can't say publicly without blowing the whole diplomatic game plan. It is true the president dressed this visit up in all the proper diplomatic, peaceful-coexistence, forgive-and-forget trappings that are so much a part of the great international chess game. It is also true that this does confuse and disturb Republicans who have believed in his hardheaded knowledge of the communists, if in nothing else. But let's look at it as a move in a very dangerous game where the stakes are freedom itself. You and I know that a president of the United States can really and practically no longer pursue the policy of peripheral containment of communism. American public opinion will no longer tolerate wars of the Vietnam type, because they no longer feel a threat, thanks to the ɪ ̲ ̲ ̲ ̲ ̲ ̲ ̲ess, from communism, and they cannot interpret thoꜱꜱ ꜱ's as being really in the defense of freedom and our own country.

"Russia is still enemy number one. Russia is the country that very shortly will have the power to deliver an ultimatum. So the president, knowing of the disaffection between China and Russia, visits China, butters up the warlords, and lets them be, because they have nothing to fear from us. Russia, therefore, has to keep its 140 divisions on the Chinese border; hostility between the two is increased; and we buy a little time and elbowroom in a plain, simple strategic move, a million miles removed from the soft appeasement of previous Democratic administrations."

Reagan's support of the American presence in South Vietnam brough unhappy letters from some. One, from a young naval ensign, brought these thoughts in reply: "I can't help but think that the things you see today and which are disturbing to you, and certainly to all of us, are not the result of America being where it shouldn't be, but possibly the result of America forsaking its principles several years ago by asking men to fight and die for a cause that by some strange reasoning we said, at the same time, was not a cause worth winning."

He pointed out that "War very often brings out the noblest in men. By the same token, particularly when it drags on the way this has with no apparent goal in sight, it can

bring out the worst. I fear very much this has happened.
All I would suggest is, not that you lose your repugnance
for the evils you see around you, but that you not let that
distort your thinking with regard to the rightness or wrong-
ness of America's position in the war against totalitarian
aggression. Very simply, that is what this conflict is all
about. It is not America who has said we seek to impose
our will on the world. It is the communist combine subscribing to the ideology of Karl Marx, which has said we
will not be satisfied until we have imposed our way on the
entire wor'

In his letter the governor did not hesitate to contrast the
Republicans to the Democrats. In one to Thomas B. Meek
of Santa Barbara he wrote: "All the potential Democratic
candidates for president are saying the same thing in almost
identical terms: 'Turn the country around—change direction.' Do they really mean that? Or do they mean, stop the
change in direction and return to the eight years of Camelot
and the Great Society, when we talked of long hot summers
and accepted burning cities and rioting campuses as a matter
of course, a way of life? They mired us down in a land war
in Asia, doubled the budget, and ran the national debt up
by seventy billion dollars—more than the combined debt
of all the nations of the world. Inflation doubled and quad-
rupled, and we didn't let ourselves think how close we were
to carrying our money in a basket. They declared war on
poverty and couldn't win that one either.

"Somehow, a myth has gained wide acceptance that our
opponents are the party of good times and prosperity. Many
of our sons and daughters have been spoon-fed this myth
in too many social science courses. These young people
complain of regimentation by an impersonal bureaucratic
government, of unsolved problems of human misery, and
of war. And then, with a distorted perspective of history,
we are told they are registering two to one in the party that
presided over all these things. It is time to expose the myth;
time to tell our sons and daughters we, too, are against
these things; time to let them know we weren't running the
shop when all this came into being.

"A Republican president has occupied the White House

only eleven of the last forty years, and in only one two-year term did a Republican president have a Republican congress. This was the only two-year period in which the dollar did not depreciate in value. We have known four wars in my lifetime, all under Democratic administrations. And in the last forty years the only time we have known full employment, it has been the result of one of these wars. After six years of the New Deal, twenty-five percent of our workers were unemployed. World War II brought full employment. The next time, it was the war in Korea. A Republican president ended that one, and for eight years no young American was asked to die for his country.

"Now another Republican president is ending another war. In the transition to a peacetime economy there is a certain dislocation. Two million former servicemen and defense workers have joined the labor pool, and so we have temporary unemployment. Three hundred young Americans are not dying each and every week in a far away jungle. It would seem that unemployment, like wine, has vintage years. Today it is a crisis. We are told we are in a recession and, yet, unemployment is no higher today than it was during all those three years of Camelot. But then unemployment was taken for granted. In two years of frequent press conferences, President Kennedy was never asked once if he intended doing anything about unemployment. Only when they revved up to a full-scale war in Vietnam did we have full employment.

"The Democratic myth is built on false claims and a denial of reality. For thirty-eight of the last forty years, this nation's policy has largely been determined by a Democratic leadership which long ago abandoned the principles of Jefferson and Jackson.

"Today millions of Democrats and our own sons and daughters seek a course to believe in. There is a hunger today for spiritual values. Our people yearn to believe in their country and in themselves. Let that be our cause."

In a letter to a corporate executive he explained why he had become opposed to allowing corporations to contribute to campaigns: "I have become alarmed at a fairly recent development in the political process, namely the support—

usually unreported by organized labor and government-employee organizations. In 1968 C.O.P.E. spent $68 million on the Humphrey campaign and only about $15 million had to be reported as contribution. The ruling group of our state employee's association this year announced they were going to contribute $500,000 to the candidate for governor who would 'do the most for them.'

"Yet in the 'Watergate' hysteria we see 'business' attacked as the source of all evil and curbs suggested on corporations but not on union practices. I don't believe there is any way to curb labor except by a blanket rule. Furthermore, labor's contributions do not reflect the actual preferences of the rank and file. Indeed many union members are compelled to support candidates who are not their choice. There is no way that even the biggest corporate givers can match this abuse of the democratic process by labor.

"I hope corporations and unions will urge their people—employees, stockholders, customers, and members to vote and contribute, and even which way to vote and contribute, but let's halt a handful of labor bosses from acting as power brokers in the name of millions of constituents who aren't even consulted as to their wishes.

"Incidentally, I will oppose to the end public funding of campaigns. We are agreed on the danger inherent in that."

Not all of the governor's unfriendly letters were from political enemies, as we have seen. By the same token some of his political enemies wrote friendly letters.

Bob Moretti, then speaker of the assembly, reacted to a personal attack on the governor, with a handwritten letter that began, "This is a very harsh business sometimes. There are occasions, however, when people go too damn far in attempting to make the other fellow look bad; I don't like it when it happens to me and I'm sure you feel the same.

". . . when a government official is attacked without reason it's unfair to him, his family, and all who are taken in by it. I'm sorry this happened."

The governor responded, "Just a quick line to tell you how very much I appreciate the note you had delivered to me over the weekend. You were kind to write as you did, and I'm most grateful.

"Sometimes I get concerned, not just with attacks on ourselves as individuals, but what we may be doing to the very structure of government. It seems lately there has been a growing disrespect, not for the officeholder so much as for the office itself, whether that be in the legislative or in the executive branch. This could pose a great danger to everything that I think we both want."

Another personal attack on the governor brought a strange and touching exchange of correspondence between him and Representative Jerome Waldie, a California Democrat.

Waldie had attacked the governor for his unfortunate remark—yes, even Ronald Reagan slips once in a while— that "It's just too bad we can't have an epidemic of botulism" in the food distribution program brought about by the Patty Hearst kidnapping.

The governor explained publicly that the statement "was made at a completely private gathering. I used a very ludicrous statement to simply express the frustration."

Waldie, however, who was in the midst of a losing campaign for the Democratic nomination for governor, refused to accept the explanation. In a public statement of his own, Waldie said that "insensitive, heavy-handed ugly attempts at humor on the part of the governor . . . must only add to the dangers Patty Hearst is already experiencing. I don't expect the governor to understand the problems and the tragedy of poor and hungry people, but surely he must recognize that his irresponsible comments endanger Patty Hearst. Governor, keep quiet, please."

That remark brought this letter from the governor:

"Dear Jerry:

"Ordinarily, I wouldn't write a letter like this in reply to a public statement, and if you've been misquoted in the attached article, ignore this one. In case the article is accurate, however, I'm writing because of late I've become increasingly concerned about the harshness with which all of us seem to react with regard to our differences.

"I realize that you and I approach our jobs from a different philosophical viewpoint and, yet, in times past men of good will could disagree, debate their differences, and do so without the animus that characterizes today's political rhetoric.

"You assail me for 'insensitivity and endangering Patty Hearst' and yet I have scrupulously refrained from public comment and have explained to the press at every opportunity my reasons for not answering their questions. The remark of mine you are quoted as saying was 'ugly, heavy-handed humor' was, as the news story indicates, uttered in a private gathering and certainly not as a joke. I find nothing to joke about in this terrible and tragic situation.

"It was one of those exaggerations we all at times utter to express frustration and we do so with the confidence that no one takes us literally. How often do we say 'I'd like to tear him limb for limb' or 'I'd give a million dollars,' etc.?

"Some individual, however, for his own purposes, felt compelled to phone a single reporter who then proceeded to publicize my unfortunate choice of words. I can only assume that he placed a greater importance on embarrassing me than on protecting a kidnap victim.

"You then (if you are correctly quoted) go on to say that you don't expect me to understand the problems and the tragedy of the poor and hungry people. This is an example of the political rhetoric I mentioned. Jerry, I assume we all want to help the less fortunate as well as all our citizens—that's why we are in public life—or at least it should be our reason.

"I don't know too much about your background and obviously you don't know much about mine except for the widely publicized occupation I once was in. But let me assure you I do understand the 'problems and the tragedy of poor and hungry people.' I grew up as one of them. Knowing poverty at first hand has left me deeply imbued with a belief that opening opportunities for the poor to improve their lot is the only acceptable solution to this greatest of all human miseries.

"Handouts at the price of a young girl's life are not an answer—we'd soon run out of young girls. Obviously, we must provide for all who need help, but we should do so always with the conviction we are doing this as a stopgap until we can make them self-sustaining. Seven years ago, California's labor department was ineffectual—unwanted by job hunters or those who offered employment. Last year we found jobs for 275,000 Californians; 59,000 of them were welfare recipients. In the last six months of this fiscal year we have already moved 37,000 welfare people into private-industry jobs.

"The two-party system should be like our variety of churches—we are all headed in the same direction, we just have different ways of getting there."

And this response from Waldie:

"Dear Governor:

"You are quite right in your gentle admonition to me concerning the excessive rhetoric I used in responding to your reported off-the-record remarks about botulism.

"I know you are not insensitive and I know you care. I also believe your personal childhood experiences must have made the impact on your views of the necessity of assisting the poor that you describe.

"I am sorry, Governor. We can all do better in this process and you were correct in noting my deficiencies in this regard.

"Your letter was a touching and a moving one. We should all develop the grace in responding to an injustice that you exhibited in that letter.

"I don't know if you desire to release my apology publicly, but be assured that I would have absolutely no objections in your doing so.

"Thank you, Governor, for helping me toward understanding."

The Spirit of the Man

Ronald Reagan is a sensitive man, perceptive, and with an instinctive kindness in his make-up. He is also unashamedly moral and deeply religious. He has a strong belief that the Lord's will plays a part in the affairs of men and that faith in the Lord is essential if a man is to achieve great things.

He expressed his faith succinctly in a 1976 letter to Dorothy D. Conaghan of Tonkawa, Oklahoma. "I have come to realize that whatever I do has meaning only if I ask that it serves His purpose. . . . I believe that in my present undertaking (he was then a candidate for president), whatever the outcome, it will be His doing. I will pray for understanding of what it is He would have me do.

"I have long believed there was a divine plan that placed this land here to be found by people of a special kind that we have a rendezvous with destiny. Yes, there is a spirit moving in this land and a hunger in the people for a spiritual revival.

"If the task I seek should be given me, I would pray only that I could perform it in a way that would serve God."

It is this faith which sometimes approaches fatalism that not only is one of the governor's greatest strengths but also is a trait that frustrates some of his associates who from time to time worry that nice guys don't always finish first.

The following letters and excerpts say much more about

the governor's religious beliefs, personal philosophy, and approach to life.

In a letter to Billy Graham he wrote that, "Like you, I walk between that pessimism expressed by your congress-man and newspaper friends and my own optimism based on faith."

Continuing, he turned to a discussion of some of today's religious trends. "For a long time now I have been opposed to the young people's rejection of the church; at the same time they seem to be turning to Christ. Now I wonder if they haven't sensed something in advance of the rest of us. It fills me with terror to think of seminaries turning out class after class of clergymen who, apparently, are more social worker than minister, and to read of an entire de-nomination teaching young people to approach the Bible with their own beliefs as to what they should and should not accept."

Then he added, "It has always seemed to me that Christ in His own words gave us reason to accept literally the miracle of His birth and resurrection. He said, 'I am the Son of God.' Indeed, He said so many things that we have a very simple choice: either we believe Him, or we must assume He was the greatest liar who ever lived. If we believe the latter, then we have to ask, could such a charlatan have had the impact on the world for two thousand years that this man has had? We have known other great fakers down through the centuries. Some are even a paragraph in history. None had a lasting effect.

"I don't think I am one who believes the church should completely abandon its concern for man's physical being, but heaven help us if the church's concern in this direction makes it forget its responsibility for our spiritual welfare. Jesus was very explicit, it seems to me, about man finding salvation in his own soul, making the determination that he personally would do good. Somehow, it seems, the church is copping out if it substitutes for conversion the coercion of government and the taxing power to make peo-ple do good through government programs, whether or not they have made the decision in their own hearts that they want to do good."

As recently as March 1, 1978, he restated his belief in the divinity of Christ. It was in response to a letter from a Methodist minister who said he admired "your willingness to testify to your faith in Jesus Christ," but then went on to say:

"For myself, I am not sure whether Jesus Christ ever declared himself Messiah or not. I am not totally sure that he was conceived by the Holy Spirit and born of a virgin, and I am not totally sure he was God Incarnate during his earthly lifetime."

Governor Reagan wrote back that statements Christ made about himself "foreclose, in my opinion, any questions as to his divinity. It doesn't seem to me that he gave us any choice; either he was what he said he was or he was the world's greatest liar. It is impossible for me to believe a liar or charlatan could have had the effect on mankind that he has had for 2000 years. We could ask, would even the greatest of liars carry his lie through the crucifixion when a simple confession would have saved him?

"Did he allow us the choice you say that you and others have made, to believe in his teachings but reject his statements about his own identity?"

In response to a letter from a woman protesting the teaching of evolution in the public schools the governor pointed out that "I can't impose a dictate on the board," but then went on to say, "Somehow I've never had any trouble reconciling spiritual and scientific versions of creation. God's miracles are to be found in nature itself; the wind and waves, the wood that becomes a tree—all of these are explained biologically, but behind them is the hand of God. And I believe that is true of creation itself."

To another constituent he wrote: "I could not bear this job for a day if I did not have an abiding faith in God and if I did not feel I could call upon Him for help. I do believe we are bound to help our less fortunate brothers. I believe also that Christ made it plain this should come from our hearts voluntarily. Indeed He resisted those who suggested that, as a king, He should order compliance."

In a letter to the Reverend John J. McVernon, of the Narcotic Addiction Control Commission at the Brooklyn,

N.Y., Central Rehabilitation Center, he discussed a meeting he had had with Pope Paul. The Pope, he said, "has been most helpful to the United States in the international effort to reduce the drug traffic."

He continued, "However, he [the Pope] was concerned about whether this alone could solve the problem. I told him of my own feeling that it could not, that it was almost like carrying water in a sieve, and that only a program that would make our young people voluntarily reject drugs could eventually do the job. I told him of the so-called 'Jesus movement' in America and how so many young people had simply turned from drugs to a faith in Jesus. As you can imagine, he was not surprised, nor should we be, for He promised that He was our salvation."

His reliance on religion came through, too, in a reply to a letter protesting present-day sexual permissiveness.

"I don't believe the answer rests with government," he wrote, "No one can legislate morality. What we need is a spiritual awakening and return to the morals of a Christian society."

In another letter in response to a question, he touched on the same subject: ". . . no, I am not supporting the movement to abolish or lessen the present laws concerning sexual conduct. I am deeply concerned with the wave of hedonism—the humanist philosophy so prevalent today—and believe this nation must have a spiritual rebirth, a rededication to the moral precepts which guided us for so much of our past, and we must have such a rebirth very soon."

But the governor was able to joke a little about the subject, also. A constituent sent him a clipping in which a state senator who favored prescribing birth control devices for teen-age girls without parental consent charged that "illegitimate births to teen-aged mothers have increased alarmingly while Reagan has been in office."

Reagan replied: "Thanks very much for sending me the clipping . . . I have never felt so young and virile." He added on a serious note that "I can't rid myself of the idea that someone should perhaps be reasoning with teen-age girls before they get pregnant, rather than throwing up our hands and trying to figure out how to eliminate the consequences of their acts."

Most people who know him agree that during his eight years as governor Ronald Reagan changed very little. Asked to write his observations on changes which occur in an individual who becomes famous, the governor responded: "I believe that a mature person will not change very much at all. This person will express the traits and attitudes in the new setting which were true before. Some individuals who become subject to considerable public attention before they have 'grown up' are less predictable. Though the same person is there as before, becoming used to a loss of privacy or to attention—deserved or sometimes less deserved—may bring about unexpected aggressiveness or shyness, unnoticed conceit or humility. I would suggest that the main question has to do with the personality, not with fame."

He penned a P.S. to the letter: "In my previous career—motion pictures—we had a truism about people who 'went Hollywood'—they always were that way. Hollywood just exposed it."

The spirit of Christian forgiveness shone through in a letter to a youth who had threatened to bomb the state capitol. The boy wrote to apologize for what he called "a prank." The governor wrote back: "I appreciate and accept your apology and do forgive you. I think I understand also something of what caused you to do what you did. You say you have learned your lesson and will never play another prank of this kind again. I hope that this is really true and that you have learned the hurt that can come from what seems to be a harmless joke.

"As the years have gone on, I have come to the conclusion that the so-called practical joke can rarely be played without someone actually being hurt, sometimes very seriously. I won't go into detail about what happens in a capitol such as ours when a threat is received but will only say in these days of terrorist activity when so many real threats and real bombings occur, the possibility of tragedy arising from a false report is very great indeed.

"Michael, we don't understand many times why some things happen in our lives, why we incur some losses. Many times, however, as the years go by, we do get some understanding and acceptance of blows which at the moment of their happening seem entirely without reason. You have a long life ahead of you. It can be a rich and full one, particularly if you decide that helping, not hurting, others is the way to go.

"Again, let me say you have not only my forgiveness, but my very best wishes for your future."

Governor Reagan expressed his deep belief that there is a divine plan in a letter to a New York woman who had written of her handicapped son. ". . . I find myself believing very deeply that God has a plan for each one of us. Some with little faith and even less testing seem to miss in their mission, or else we perhaps fail to see their imprint on the lives of others. But bearing what we cannot change and going on with what God has given us, confident there is a destiny, somehow seems to bring a reward we wouldn't exchange for any other. It takes a lot of fire and heat to make a piece of steel."

To her son he wrote: ". . . things have a way of working out in life, and usually for the best, if we simply go forward doing our best and trusting that God does have a plan.

"Your handwriting may be 'slow and wiggly,' but already you've conquered this with the typewriter. Your thinking isn't 'slow and wiggly.' All of the miracles we know in this fast-moving world have come from man's brain. Sometimes, some of us have to be forced to use our minds, and we can resent this and grow bitter, or we can go forward, trusting in a divine scheme of things. I think you've made your choice already, and the right one. Your parents must be very proud of you."

Criticism that the governor had no compassion because of some of his welfare policies always bothered him. "Naturally," he said in one letter, "I feel our administration has compassion.

"I'm sure everyone feels sorry for the individual who has fallen by the wayside or who can't keep up in our competitive society, but my own compassion goes beyond that to those millions of unsung men and women who get up every morning, send the kids to school, go to work, try to keep up the payments on their house, pay exorbitant taxes to make possible compassion for the less fortunate, and as a result have to sacrifice many of their own desires and dreams and hopes. Government owes them something better than always finding a new way to make them share the fruit of their toils with others."

But, while feeling government must be compassionate, he has never changed his view that much of what government does today could better be done by the people. In a letter to J. Harry Hargrove of Birmingham, Alabama, in September 1977, he restated his position: "We are not to have graven images, or to have any other Gods before Him. Sometimes I fear that with the best of intentions, with only a desire to help those less fortunate, we are making a god of government. A Samaritan crossed over the road and helped the beaten pilgrim himself—he did not report the case to the nearest welfare agency.

"Let us have the courage to seek out those things which government is now doing, but which we, as Christians, should be doing voluntarily. Let us have the courage that this is a nation under God and in God is our trust. Let us repudiate the permissiveness so widespread in our land today. If God has supported such a view, he would have sent Moses down from the mountain with tablets upon which were engraved the ten suggestions."

The governor also outlined a little of his philosophy of leadership in a letter to Alfred B. Hastings, Jr., of Los Angeles. "In this country of ours, we have no titled aristocracy. We do have, of course, a group of people who attain stature and prestige because of accomplishment, not through accident of birth. Our founding fathers, who gave us our start, were men of this kind who had attained stature in their communities and who felt a deep sense of responsibility. I believe their concept of what this country would be was based on a belief that there would always be men of stature who would take time out from their private lives to give service to the community, hold office in government, or contribute in other ways as a kind of repayment for the good fortune they have known. Somewhere along the line, we've lost some of that.

"I believe the time has come for a new noblesse oblige by the American aristocracy of accomplishment."

He concluded: "This country can be as great as the people were willing to make it. But those who have achieved leadership positions in the great private sector owe a little of that leadership to the community as a whole. Politics is too important to be left to politicians. The rewards are indescribable."

In another philosophical letter the governor wrote about an address he made to a group of college-age youth: "I told them probably part of our lack of communication between generations could be a resentment on our part that our sons and daughters seem to assume they and they alone desire peace. I asked them to remember that we, who had bled the finest of our generation into a thousand battlefields around the world in World War II, knew what it was to say good-bye to friends and loved ones. We had a built-in deep love and desire for peace, indeed, a hatred for war. I asked them also to ask themselves what kind of a world they would be living in if our generation had not been willing to do that, if we had not been willing to land on an Omaha Beach or a thousand atolls, or if our young men had not been willing to fight their way across the hedgerows of Normandy or the sands of Africa or up the boot of Italy.

"Each generation must learn that the things men prize the most, the things which make a civilization, are those things for which men have always been willing to die. If our generation has failed, perhaps the failure has been to teach this to our sons and daughters."

Responding to a letter attacking him which appeared in the Eureka College publication, *Pegasus*, the governor discussed a bit of his philosophy of education: "Education is not the means of showing people how to get what they want. Education is an exercise by means of which enough men, it is hoped, will learn to want what is worth having. Discipline is involved because true freedom of choice is impossible until we are sufficiently self-disciplined to know what the results of our choices will be. A society provides education to assure the continuation of the culture and moral values upon which that society is founded. It is society's attempt to enunciate certain ultimate values upon which individuals and, hence, society may safely build.

"The cynics of ancient Rome challenged every Roman value, derided every standard as middle-class prejudice, and led their students down the path of total rejection and disbelief. They were very successful, as witness the decline and fall of the Roman Empire."

Another letter had this to say about modern education: ". . . today's universities, or at least too many of the faculty, seem bent on regimenting everyone into some kind of forced equality, wherein there will be no reliance on individuals rising above the crowd."

During his years in office the governor gave his views on a wide range of subjects, such as a suggestion that officeholders' tax returns should be made public: "The risk . . . is that more and more, government is tending to pry into the personal lives of citizens and put the information gained on public display. Doing so with elected officials would be a first big step to doing it with everyone, and there goes that issue we fought for in the American Revolution; a citizen has the right of privacy on his books and papers.

"May I add one other drawback? It is hard enough now to get successful and capable people to enter into public life—this could make it almost impossible."

On the subject of bigness: ". . . just being big is not necessarily bad. It is when someone attempts to take advantage of his bigness that we must make sure the smaller fellow is protected against that aggression by superior size and muscle. Strangely enough, many of the people who decry big business . . . are the same ones who justify their lust for big government on the basis that if we're going to have big business and big labor we must have big government.

"Well, I'm opposed to monopoly, whether it be by labor, by business, or by government and I am in favor of a constant three-way attack on those monopolies. . . . I believe the biggest threat is big government, but it is supported by and feeds on big labor, and I fear that there are those in business who see a chance at monopoly, whether they use the word or not, if they go along with big government. I'm afraid the fight is never-ending, but we must continue."

On the road to peace: "If you will look back at the periods of the longest peace in our country you will find they have been those times when the United States based its international decisions and relations on sound moral principles with the firm expression that rather than sacrifice such principles we would fight.

"There are those today, I know, who believe in peace at any price. This can only be obtained if you are willing to accept slavery."

And on people-involvement: "In recent years, growing possibly from the great depression years when people were literally stunned by the collapse of the economy, there has been a decline in political participation by the people. The Roosevelt era was characterized by a government takeover to an extent we've never known. Personal initiative was our national characteristic. Organized labor was fragmented and had little power mainly because most Americans resisted joining anything that might restrict their individualism.

"The pattern changed quickly. The year I graduated from college the government was running radio ads urging you not to leave home looking for work, but to stay and wait for the government to help you.

"Today so many things we once thought of as personal or private responsibilities are now just accepted as government's job. With this, in my opinion, has grown the idea that we are incapable as individuals of affecting government. Thus the cliches—'there is no difference between the parties,' 'my vote doesn't count,' and 'politicians are all alike.'

"I have learned that the people can influence government and that our system will only work if the people participate. But the people must be informed, or rather inform themselves.

"Jefferson said the people will not make a mistake—*if* they have *all* the facts. If there is a weakness in our two-party system it is that we accept a party label as ours and then vote the label without questioning whether the party continues to represent our own philosophical beliefs.

"I was a Democrat when the Democratic party stood for states rights, local autonomy, economy in government, and individual freedom. Today it is a party that has changed, openly declaring for centralized federal power and government-sponsored redistribution of the individual's earnings.

"You asked for some ideas. Let me suggest that every government service should be weighed against the cost of that service in loss of personal freedom. We willingly give up our right to drive ninety miles an hour down a city street because we want safety for self and family. By the same token, do we want government to have the right to censor films because some film makers lack good taste?

"Government exists to protect rights which are ours from birth; the right to life, to liberty, and the pursuit of happiness. A man may choose to sit and fish instead of working—that's his pursuit of happiness. He does not have the right to force his neighbors to support him (welfare) in his pursuit because that interferes with their pursuit of happiness."

First and Last Principles

ALTHOUGH RONALD REAGAN'S interest in national affairs was often labeled "politics" rather than "concern," the truth is that during his governorship, in many ways he became the conscience of our nation because he truly and deeply cares.

Driven by the instincts of a missionary and the perceptions of a student of history who knows that we must heed the lessons of the past if we want to prevent the United States from joining the list of fallen empires, he will continue to be a strong and outspoken voice in America.

The signs of decay and decline in our country today make it plain that we desperately need men of vision, courage, and dedication. The people may not call Ronald Reagan to lead us as president, but I am sure history will record him as one man who strove in perilous times to preserve our country as a great nation.

Ronald Reagan's courage must be unquestioned. He has stood up to the toughest decisions a man in public office must make and not flinched, although, I must say, he has prayed, agonized, and sought the best advice available before deciding.

Few remember the one execution that took place in California when Ronald Reagan was governor. It was early in his administration. The condemned man had killed a po-

liceman in the course of a robbery. Yet there was strong
outcry from those opposed to capital punishment. The night
before the execution the governor met with his minister,
and the two men prayed together.

The next morning the governor heard from his legal
affairs secretary that there were just no extenuating circumstances, and he ordered the execution to proceed.

At that time there were nearly a hundred men in San
Quentin's death row because the governor's predecessor
had continually granted stays of execution. A legitimate
fear of the governor's was that he would be forced to proceed with the executions of many of them. The Supreme
Court ruling against the death penalty, however, took this
worry from him. His first execution was also his last. But
he remained, and still remains, a strong proponent of the
death penalty on the grounds that it is a deterrent to pre-
meditated murder.

Another issue involving life and death with which the
governor struggled was abortion. In a letter to Charles
Schulz, the creator of Peanuts, Governor Reagan explained
his stand. He wrote, he said, because "of one of your strips
a few weeks ago which continues to haunt me in a very nice
way."

He went on: "Charlie was asking Lucy about what happens to a very nice baby waiting in heaven to be born when
the mother and father decide they don't want it. Lucy of
course put him down severely. Charlie finished simply re-
marking he still thought it was a good question.

"Perhaps my feeling for Charlie's question stems from
the soul-searching I had to do a few years ago with regard
to the liberalizing of our abortion laws. The author of the
legislation wanted to go all the way and simply make it a
matter of personal choice and wide open. I probably did
more studying on that subject at that time than on anything
else before or since and finally had to tell him I would veto
such a bill. I could only reconcile abortion with the right
of self-defense, namely the right of the mother to protect
herself and her health against even her own unborn child
if the birth of that child threatened her. It has been my
feeling that our religion does justify the taking of life in

self-defense. I cannot accept that simply on whim even a mother has the right to take the life of her unborn child simply because she thinks that child will be born less than perfect or because she just doesn't want to be bothered. Well, the bill was amended to meet my demands and I signed it into law. Now, however, I have discovered some of our psychiatrists are particularly willing to declare an unwed mother-to-be to have suicidal tendencies, and they do this on a five-minute diagnosis. The result is that our medical program will finance more than fifty thousand abortions of unwed mothers in the coming year on such flimsy diagnosis.

"Well, I didn't mean to let you in on all my problems but just to give the background of why you touched a nerve with your strip the other day. Thanks very much."

Another letter, this to William A. Barker, professor of physics at the University of California, attested to his strong feelings in this area: "I am deeply committed to a belief in the sacredness of human life. I share your revulsion for the view expressed by your dinner companion that the human fetus is no more than an appendage to be removed as you would an appendix.

"Right now a group of distinguished jurists in the Midwest are seeking a court decision to establish the rights of the unborn child. Their brief cites recent medical research to the effect that an individual, distinct life begins at the moment of conception at which time the genetic components that determine the characteristics of a person are established. Dr. H. M. I. Lilley is quoted as saying, 'The fetus is neither an acquiescent vegetable nor a witless tadpole as some have conceived it to be in the past, but rather is a tiny human being as independent as though lying in a crib with a blanket wrapped around him.'

"I realize there is a body of thought on the other side, but it should follow that where there is doubt as to the question of life or death, the benefit of the doubt should be given to life.

"The California abortion law is based on the Judeo-Christian tradition of self-defense—the right of a woman to take a life in defense of her own. It does not permit the taking of that unborn life simply on the whim of a mother unwilling to carry and bear that child or for fear the child might be born less than perfect.

"Unfortunately, there are those professionals in California, particularly in the field of psychiatry, who are abdicating their responsibility. They are permitting abortions by falsifying as to the mother's risk—claiming self-defense when, in fact, there is no danger. This is as false as claiming self-defense in the murder of a victim who was unarmed and who posed no threat to his killer. You are right to equate this with Hitlerism. How far are we from killing for convenience the unwanted among us if we accept killing them in the womb?"

The governor was dismayed at how the California abortion law was distorted and finally all but rendered void by a ruling of the state supreme court. A letter to Mrs. Win Robin   of Los Angeles displayed his feelings: "California's abortion law *was* based on the rule of self-defense—the right of a woman to protect herself from harm even at the hand of her own unborn child. Provisions for medical review were included in the act to make certain the abortion was necessary to the mother's safety. There is no question but that many, particularly in the field of psychiatry, failed in this responsibility.

"Now the Supreme Court of California has ruled such protective measures need not be applied. I personally think the decision was a license to murder and that we are committing murder on a wholesale scale."

Finally he wrote to Dr. Mildred F. Jefferson of Boston, Massachusetts, a strong opponent of abortion who had appeared on a television show, "The Advocates." "I am disturbed, as you may be, by public-opinion polls showing an almost equal division in the country on this subject. I find it hard to believe that the essentially moral people of this country could in such numbers support abortion on demand unless it is that they are tragically uninformed on the subject.

"I have been meeting with groups of young people in question-and-answer sessions hoping that by such a free exchange they could get a better understanding of government and many of the issues of our time. Invariably, this subject comes up; and here, too, I find that overwhelmingly these young people never give consideration to the human-life aspect but are convinced that abortion is a necessary aid in controlling the birth rate and preventing the birth of unwanted children who will then, according to their belief, live tragic lives.

"I had a touching experience in one such meeting with students from five high schools who had come here to the capitol. One young lady spoke quite eloquently about the fate of the unwanted child after it had been born. I pointed out to them that there were literally millions of people in this country who could not have children and who were lined up waiting, many times for years, to adopt babies that are just not being born now.

"As the session ended, a very pretty, wholesome-looking, fresh-faced young lady sort of tentatively raised her hand; and I took her question as the last that we had time for—I'm glad I did. She said, 'I am adopted. I care very much for my folks; I'm sure they care for me.' And then she added this line. She said, 'I'm glad someone didn't kill me.' I wish we could have that particular little scene on television."

The subject of abortion brings up the subject of birth control and the controversial issue of whether teen-age girls should be prescribed birth control pills or contraceptive devices without parental consent. Here are excerpts of one letter Governor Reagan wrote on the subject to a woman who had told him, "when it comes to an issue such as illegitimacy and avoidance of abortions you make unfortunate decisions and veto legislation designed to lessen illegitimacy and abortions."

". . . what we are really at odds about," the governor responded, "is not finding the solution to the individual's personal tragedy after the mistake has been made and what is the proper course to reduce or hopefully eliminate this cause of the tragedy to begin with.

"I could not have worked in the motion picture industry for most of my adult life and been a 'blue-nose' or prude. Still I have to believe that all law is based on natural law.

On the higher law of morality we know that premarital sex
or promiscuity in our entire Judeo-Christian tradition is a
sin. Most of our common law is based on this concept and
belief. In recent years an adult society has said to our young
people in a thousand different ways, including the classroom
and the lecture hall, that this concept has somehow become
outmoded and, therefore, sex ranks with the physical ap-
petites with no more importance assigned to it than eating
a ham sandwich when you're hungry. We have, in fact,
been preaching or at least accepting hedonism, and not for
the first time in man's history. The easy way, of course,
is to accept this as a new life-style and adjust accordingly.
The more difficult, but I believe proper course dictated by
the past, is to return to standards we know are based on
solid moral principles. All of history proves that happiness
is to be found by following such moral precepts.

"As I said before, I wish I knew the correct answer to
all of this. I believe it does lie in education but perhaps the
education must begin with the parent. Certainly we have
never done a good job in home teaching of our young people
about sex. I can't say that I received a scientific dissertation
on this at home but on the other hand, I did receive what
I now recognize was good, sound moral teaching. You see
at close hand the tragedy of the young girl and boy who
break the rules and then are faced with the consequences.
I see the larger problem of trying to find a way to reverse
the hedonism while at the same time having full compassion
for those young people who in spite of all teaching are
going to make mistakes. How do we do this without seem-
ingly having society put a stamp of approval on hedonism
and, in effect, eliminating the notion entirely that the young
people have made a mistake? Sex is not a purely physical
act. It has deep psychological side effects. It is indeed at
the very foundation of our social fabric based on the family
unit.

"Part of my resistance also is now based on my view
from the inside of government. I think the American people
are totally unaware of how dependent they have become on
government for making all decisions, regulating even this
very intimate facet of family life. Government is not that

omnipotent. Government would do a great service for the people if it would unwind its bureaucracy, reduce its size and wean the people and put them back on their own two feet. [I don't mean] that they have to be totally independent of all others but let them find solutions to their problems in such areas as the church, local schools, and Parent-Teacher Associations instead of having them automatically turn to a bureaucrat in some government agency or a legislator in a belief that they can make a determination that will solve all their problems. To sum it up, what problem do we make for the parent who is intelligently trying to teach moral principles to a child when government by way of the school system or whatever agency goes to the contrary and says to the child, 'Here, we know you are going to do these things regardless of what your parents say, so we'll teach you how to get away with it no harm done.'"

Virtually all the problems of human misery and suffering eventually come before any governor of our largest state. Hunger is one of those problems and it is one that is drawing increasing international attention. But like most world problems it is often distorted and seldom understood.

In a letter to Kip Hayden, editor-in-chief of the Eureka College publication, *Pegasus,* Governor Reagan discussed the broad aspects of the problem: "I was very interested in your remarks about the world food situation and the organization you spoke of. I must confess I am not too optimistic about the many world meetings that are being held on hunger. It seems that most of them come up with a very simple, but inadequate answer. The United States representatives sit there, feeling a little guilty because we've been able to feed ourselves, and the rest of the world says, 'Feed us, too.' I realize that many of us have a guilt feeling because, as is so frequently pointed out, the United States has 6 percent of the world's population and consumes 30 percent of the world's goods. This, however, is a misuse of statistics. We also produce 48 percent of the world's goods and our agricultural exploits are the greatest of any nation in the world. The greatest technological revolution in world history hasn't really been in space or any of the other exotic industries, but in American farming. We produce more food for more people with less labor and fewer workers in the field of agriculture than any other nation on earth.

"For many years I have been critical of foreign aid, not because of its intent or goal, but because I believe we have been violating the old admonition that to give a hungry man a fish is to know he'll be hungry tomorrow. To teach him how to fish will ensure he'll never be hungry again. Foreign aid over these past decades should have concentrated less on actual food distribution abroad and more on the export of American farming know-how. I still think that is a good idea in the present world situation, although now, of course, we have need for the export of food also, because of the emergency situation in so many areas.

"I have been struck by the absence of national leadership in mobilizing the people of America for efforts that used to be quite commonplace a few decades ago. For example, when the people of America, in a private undertaking but with the cooperation of the national government, saved the starving in Belgium after World War I. A similar effort took place a few years later on the occasion of the Tokyo earthquake, and this was the manner in which people of America went to the aid of others in catastrophes of one kind or another all over the world.

"This brings me to your program of gleaning, such as the corn harvest and then the corn remaining in the field. There are a million opportunities for private saving of food, not only the corn crop, but virtually every harvested crop, particularly the tree crops which leave great amounts that can be gleaned and used to help others.

"But let me point out some other areas. They may sound small, or even a little silly, but I believe there is great potential for saving in them. Four of us had breakfast together in a leading hotel recently and the butter arrived in two dishes, not in the usual pats, but dipped out with ice cream scoops. There was also a basket of bread and toast, etc. No one had asked for this so it was just put on the table as a matter of course. I noted that none of the four of us touched either the butter or the bread. Now, under our health laws, when that is returned from the table it is garbage. It cannot be served to anyone else. Two ice cream scoops of butter and a basket of bread. Would it be too difficult, in this time of shortages, for public eating places to ask first whether bread or butter is desired? Once these things are put on the table, again as I say—and properly so, our health laws require that the food cannot be served to anyone else.

"Banquets are a part of my present job. I've been interested lately to look up and down the head table and note how many times a roll and butter are placed at every setting. I've also noted how few of us eat rolls and butter with our dinner. Again, all that is left must be thrown away.

"I agree with you that we must meet our home problems first. I do disagree that there is widespread hunger in America. This is a fallacy promoted for what reasons I don't know, but actually more than 85 percent of the people of America receive the daily minimum requirement of nutrients, and I am sure that most of the remaining few percent only fail to do so because of ignorance about nutritional standards. This isn't to say there aren't some who fall through the cracks of all of our various programs and do actually experience hunger, and we should continue to do something about this."

The issue of farm labor and particularly Cesar Chavez was a continuing one during the governor's two terms. In one letter the governor wrote, "My position regarding Chavez is well known: the workers must be allowed to vote by secret ballot as to whether they should have a bargaining representative and who or what that representative should be. There can be no morality in either the boycott or in employers and Chavez signing contracts unless and until the workers themselves have voted."

Chavez' efforts to boycott California grapes, wines, and lettuce not handled by his union brought a revealing exchange of correspondence between Governor Reagan and Democratic Governor Milton J. Shapp of Pennsylvania. It began when Shapp, in an effort to help Chavez, issued a directive ordering "all state departments, boards, commissions and agencies [to] cease purchasing Iceburg lettuce."

That directive brought this letter from Reagan:

"Dear Milt:

"A copy of your directive to your state departments ordering them to cease purchasing Iceburg lettuce from Arizona and California has been brought to my attention.

"This comes as a shock to me, especially the statement that 'The United Farm Workers, in their efforts to help seasonal and migrant farm workers to better their conditions have begun a boycott of Iceburg lettuce.'

"I know that a boycott against 'nonunion' lettuce from California was endorsed at the 1972 Democratic presidential nominating convention.

"The truth is that more than 85 percent of all Iceburg lettuce grown in California and Arizona is harvested under union contracts. Only a very small percentage is produced by nonunion workers.

"There are around 170 Teamsters Union contracts in lettuce in the two states, and the United Farm Workers have only four such contracts. All of the Teamsters contracts are as valid as the UFW contracts, and members of the Teamsters Union have far better fringe benefits than do members of UFW.

"The lettuce boycott was inspired by a jurisdictional dispute between Cesar Chavez, who would like to force the growers through a boycott to break their contracts, and the Teamsters Union. Chavez would like all of those contracts turned over to him. For any state to be a party to such a jurisdictional dispute is questionable, to say the least.

"For your information, lettuce crews working in California this year are earning from $5.70 to $7.41 per hour on a piece-rate basis. During the twelve months ending May 31, 1972, farm employees in the Salinas Valley, which grows the biggest part of Iceberg lettuce, averaged $3.07 per hour. This was a composite average of piece rates, hourly, and hourly plus incentive-pay rates, with hourly guarantee jobs, and did not include foremen or salaried workers.

"The U.S. Department of Labor has recommended to all the states ten protective laws for farm workers. California has nine of those laws in effect, and the same table indicates that Pennsylvania has only six.

"The average pay of all hired farm workers in California in April of this year was $2.27 per hour; Pennsylvania's average farm-worker pay in 1971 was $1.68 per hour.

"From these facts, it would appear that Pennsylvania should be concerned about its own farm workers rather than taking punitive action against California's lettuce growers and workers, who enjoy the best working conditions for farm workers in the United States.

"It would be more appropriate to undertake a greater degree of cooperation among states rather than to engage in this dispute."

Governor Shapp replied:

"Dear Ron:

"I have read with a great deal of interest your letter of September 27th asking me in effect to mind my own business in regard to the attempts of Cesar Chavez to gain fair treatment for his people.

"This is exactly what I am doing. I am minding my own business.

"As an individual, I am greatly disturbed by the plight of the poor people in this nation, and the oppressive forces that keep them down.

"As a governor, I am trying to do something to help solve the social and economic ills that beset my state and the nation so that the American dream can be fulfilled not just by a comparative handful of wealthy people, but by all our citizens.

"Lettuce today has replaced grapes as a symbol, just as grapes at one time had quietly replaced the 'union label' as a symbol for obtaining fair treatment for labor.

"Cesar Chavez is attempting to accomplish for his people what Eugene Debs did for the railroad workers, what John L. Lewis did for the miners, what Philip Murray did for the steelworkers, what Dubinsky did for the needle trade workers, what Samuel Gompers did for the cigar makers, what Walter Reuther did for the auto workers, and yes, what James Hoffa did for the truck drivers. All of these great labor leaders gave the working men and women of America a chance to work under safe conditions, at fair wages, and to be treated with dignity.

"Throughout its turbulent history, the labor movement in America has always been opposed by those who have considered material values more important than human values.

"At one time in your career you were part of the movement to help those at the bottom reach out for daylight. But once you achieved personal success, you seemed to have changed. That was your privilege.

"But it is still my privilege to do my job as I see it.

"I believe strongly that this nation cannot achieve the goals it espouses until and unless its leaders work to help all the people, not just the privileged few.

"I believe strongly that it is your responsibility as a governor, just as it is mine, to use all the powers at our disposal to constantly fight to correct the wrongs that exist within our society to the end that this nation can indeed exist under God, with liberty and justice for all.

"Perhaps this may sound kind of corny to some, but it never sounds corny to me when I pledge allegiance to our flag.

"Pennsylvania farmers are not being harmed by the boycott of Iceburg lettuce. They are being helped to the extent that they have a greater opportunity to sell native-grown lettuce to our institutions.

"But more importantly, if all Pennsylvania citizens join with the millions of other Americans to support the present effort of Cesar Chavez, then all our people will benefit because another group of the downtrodden will be helped in the untiring effort to achieve a dignified way of life for all people.

"Ron, I shall continue to do my job as I see it—to fight constantly to help all Pennsylvania citizens obtain greater value from government for their tax dollars, to promote consumer-oriented programs, and to improve the quality of life for all our citizens.

"We have great financial and material resources in this nation, and we have great human talent.

"There is nothing that the leaders of this nation cannot accomplish for our people once we stop giving lipservice to our oft-stated principles and put our hearts and muscles behind humanely oriented, realistic programs.

"I'll mind my business in Pennsylvania. Good luck to you in California."

And this brought a last response from Governor Reagan: "Dear Milt:

"I was touched by your eloquent and moving letter; so much so that I would like to offer a constructive suggestion.

"First, however, so that you'll have no question as to my sincere interest, may I correct a misapprehension on your part? You indicated a belief that while I had served the cause of organized labor for a time, my views changed to the point of losing my capacity for compassion as I became 'better off.'

"The Screen Actors Guild (an AFL-CIO union) has a proud tradition of service to its members by working actors who for the most part have a certain individual bargaining power and really don't need union representation. Among those who have served as president were Eddie Cantor, Jimmy Cagney, Robert Montgomery, George Murphy, Walter Pidgeon, and Charlton Heston, to name a few.

"My own six terms as president were during a time when I had achieved stardom and was probably at the height of my career and my earning power.

"As I pointed out in my last letter, 85 percent of California lettuce is presently harvested by unionized labor (International Teamsters) and the salary scale is somewhat higher here than in other states. I'm sure you would like to see all the states reach parity with California.

"My suggestion therefore is that you persuade the agriculture industry of your state to invite Cesar Chavez to come and organize the farm workers of Pennsylvania. This is a sacrifice California is prepared to make in the interest of human compassion and I assure you, thousands of our own farm workers—particularly those citizens of Mexican heritage—will courageously, and I might even say happily, carry on without him.

"Your own citizens will once again enjoy the taste of

Iceburg lettuce from California and Californians will feel the urge to purchase the products of Pennsylvania."

The governor sent a copy of his first letter to Shapp to Governor Jack Williams of Arizona, which inspired a note in return:

"Dear Ron:

"Really appreciated your letter of September 27th addressed to our dear friend The Honorable Milton J. Shapp.

"It occurs to me that if we're going to start this interesting exercise, Arizona and California should begin boycotting social workers, Vista workers, Ph.D's, dangerous insects, and other such items crossing our state line from Pennsylvania.

"I should imagine at this point William Penn is revolving rapidly in his grave.

"Best regards."

Another governor, Robert Ray of Iowa, sent Reagan a clipping of a news story which reported that "the Texas Senate voted a resolution of praise for farm worker organizer Cesar Chavez."

Reagan wrote back: "Thanks very much for sending me the clipping about Cesar Chavez and the Texas Senate. It makes me realize how true is the old saying, 'No man's life or property is safe while the legislature is in session.'

"Why do you suppose it is that we just never will ask those who have been there. We've had several years of Mr. Chavez here in California, and we find he neither represents the people he claims to represent, nor does he apparently have any intention of bettering their lot, and certainly he is not nonviolent. His terror tactics easily match those of the oldtime night riders in the South. Incidentally, he's the only man I've ever known who can go on a fast and gain weight.

"Last spring in an effort to resolve this situation out here, I offered the state's help in holding, once and for all, secret ballot elections whereby the workers in the fields could vote on whether they wanted union representation and if so which union. The workers were in favor, the farmers agreed to abide by the decision, and the holdout that made it impossible was Cesar Chavez.

"When the grape boycott was at its height, and some mayors like our own John Lindsay were joining the boycott, I issued invitations to mayors all over the country to come to California as our guests and see for themselves. The only one who accepted the invitation was the young mayor of Vancouver, British Columbia. They're fairly well socialized there and he evidently leaned that way, including a bias toward Chavez. But he arrived, went into the fields, met with the workers in the fields, traced every rumor and story for himself, and walked down the picket lines. After four days he told the press of California there would be no boycott of grapes in his city. He said he had found no workers in the fields who wanted to join Chavez' union and he found no pickets on the picket lines who were farm workers.

"Well, this is little thanks for your good letter to make you put up with such a diatribe. As you've guessed, I've had my fill of Mr. Chavez and now I've had my fill of the Texas Senate. Spare both our states from such."

A former governor with whom Governor Reagan had occasion to correspond was his predecessor, Edmund G. "Pat" Brown, Sr. Brown, although known as an amiable man, has always resented his defeat at the hands of an "actor," and the bitterness shows through from time to time. A Republican fundraising letter signed by the governor was sent to Brown by mistake. This kind of mistake is common when computerized mass mailings are used, but the former governor took the opportunity to respond snidely. The fundraising letter made another mistake common to computers and addressed him as "Dear Hon. Brown:" because it was addressed to Hon. (instead of Mr.) Edmund G. Brown and the computer was programmed to pick up the title and the last name.

Brown wrote back:

"Dear Hon. Reagan:

"In today's mail I received a letter from you recalling the days of the Brown-Unruh clique.

"I am very interested in your record of increased taxation, increased welfare costs, and property taxes.

"I really believe that Edmund G. Brown, Jr., will do a

far better job than your hand-picked candidate, Houston Flournoy. I must, therefore, refuse your kind invitation to contribute to the Republican State Central Committee.

"Sincerely,

"Edmund G. Brown"

Chuckling all the while, the governor penned a short reply:

"Dear Pat:

"I just thought you might be ready to do penance."

As he points out from time to time, Governor Reagan was active in his own union, the Screen Actors Guild, in which he served six terms as president. Even so, many conservatives are surprised when they discover he is not a strong advocate of right-to-work laws. Many union members are also surprised. In a letter to David Y. Denholm, executive assistant to the president of Californians for Right to Work, Reagan explained: "You and I are in agreement about many things with regard to the rights of rank-and-file union members which must be protected. At the same time, however, my own experience as a union member, officer, and several times president, has convinced me these matters can be corrected within the union shop framework. (You'll note I didn't say closed shop.)"

But, although a believer in unionism, the governor is an even stronger believer in less government interference in the private sector and in "the coercive redistribution of wealth."

He writes in a letter to George L. Browning of Van Nuys, California. "The less government that I advocate . . . refers to the flood of restrictive regulations spawned by recent congressional acts which have added, for example, paperwork to the small businessmen of America that requires some 130 million man-hours at a cost of $50 billion simply to fill out government forms which then are shuffled and reshuffled in Washington at another expense of some $20 billion. I have no intention of suggesting that we eliminate those time-tested regulations which are necessary to protect us from the unscrupulous—for example, the pure food laws. . . .

"You suggest it is bigotry to criticize those practices of

socialist or communist countries. I believe the danger of people in America getting the idea such practices might be good here requires a warning that a loss of individual freedom we've never experienced would go with the adoption of such practices. I am opposed also to the coercive redistribution of wealth in our free economy by government fiat. On the other hand, I have, in a number of speeches, advocated a distribution based on our capitalistic practice that there are ways to increase the ownership of our industry to the point that the majority of our workers could have not only their salary but the income derived from sharing ownership in the industries in which they work. I believe there are ways, and I have suggested some, where this could be done without taking away that which someone else owns.

"As for the unmet needs in our society which you referred to, all of those I think can better be met by a general increase in the productivity of our land and in a broader-based prosperity than through the bureaucracy of government.

"The cooperation of government, of industry, and of labor to find a way in which capitalism can be made more general, with the bulk of our people participating in individual ownership—not the collective ownership by way of government that is advocated by some and practiced in some countries—is necessary."

His opposition to a particular tax proposition on the 1972 ballot brought many letters of protest. In response to one he declared: "The plain truth is, for many, many years we have all been lied to about taxing business and thus reducing the individual's tax burden. There is no way that business can be made to pay a tax. Business collects taxes, and if businesses cannot include all of their taxes as production expenses in the price of their product, they go out of business. There are 116 business taxes, so-called, in the price of a suit of clothes. All such taxes are passed on to the ultimate consumer—the individual citizen. The real problem with taxes in our country is simply the high cost of government, and taxes cannot be lowered until the people hold government more accountable. Now, who is the real villain in that picture? Out of your tax dollar the federal government gets seventy cents. The state government is run on about seven cents of that dollar, and the rest goes for schools and local and county governments."

The prospect of adding regional governments at either the federal or state levels is a real concern to many Americans. The governor answered one letter on this subject, in part: "The president [Nixon] from the first has sought to decentralize the Washington bureaucrats and get more authority and decision-making back to state and local governments. To this end he regionalized a number of federal agencies to lessen decision-making in Washington and to give the states an ability to resolve issues without taking on the Washington bureaucracy."

For his own part, he said, ". . . while I recognize there will be problems mutual to several communities, it is my belief any regional approach to those problems should be made by the elected representatives of those communities. I do not favor the creation of any additional layer of government."

The energy crisis also brought letters and responses. To Maxwell H. Smith of Malibu, California, he wrote: "I think before we tee off on the oil industry itself, we had better look at the record regarding warnings coming from that industry about this present shortage. In 1960 the American Association of Petroleum Geologists met at a convention in Los Angeles and predicted that by 1975 the United States would be in exactly the situation we're in now. They added these words, 'When it happens they will blame the industry and say, why didn't you warn us; well, we're warning you now.'

"As to the other matter, for a long time I have firmly believed the answer to all our waste problems was finding a use for them. It's all well and good to post signs saying, 'do not litter,' but if the litter becomes too valuable to throw away the problem is solved. I think you will be reassured to know that we have a pilot plant right now that has discovered that it can make oil from garbage. A little more atmosphere-polluting than petroleum, but still an oil that can be used, perhaps where pollution is not such a problem. We also have discovered, and are running a pilot plant, making oil from the rice hulls we used to burn. What is even more exciting, I think, is the discovery that we can convert sludge and decaying garbage to methane gas which can be used to generate electricity.

"I think the Arabs did us a favor by bringing the issue to a head; they didn't cause our problems, for we were on our way to this shortage even with their oil, but now perhaps we'll go forward and find the other fuel sources that will make all our throwaways useful."

The governor occasionally answered letters addressed to his wife on pertinent governmental issues. One had to do with amnesty. "I hope you won't mind my answering your letter to Mrs. Reagan, but it just seemed simpler for me to write rather than relay the information through her," he wrote. And continued: "Very simply it boils down to this: we are a nation governed by law, not men. This is the great protector of our freedom, in contrast to the days of kings (or modern-day dictators) wherein a ruler decided for or against someone by his own whim. With our freedom, of course, goes a responsibility to see that the law is upheld.

"In this case the law requires that we all serve our country when the duly-elected government decides the national policy requires such service. There has never been a war in our history when *all* our citizens agreed with the government's decision, yet the majority always abided by the law, knowing that we cannot have an orderly society if individuals can pick and choose the laws they will obey.

"Today some people are saying that because some young men considered the war immoral and avoided the draft or deserted, they should be able to return to America with no penalty now that the war is over. This, of course, is to say they should be allowed to break the law without fear of penalty.

"It is also being said that we have always granted such amnesty after previous wars. This is not true. Dating back to President Washington and the 'Whiskey Rebellion,' there has *never* been an unconditional amnesty for draft dodgers or deserters."

After tracing the record of amnesty grants by various presidents, the governor concluded: "If today's deserters are willing to return acknowledging their guilt, willing to stand trial and accept the court's decision, then amnesty could be granted on an individual basis, just as it is granted at times to other types of lawbreakers."

The United States' positions on two small foreign nations have been controversial over the years. Regarding Israel, Governor Reagan wrote to Mr. and Mrs. D. E. Matus of California: "I believe the United States is *and should be* committed to the preservation of Israel. I am convinced this is the policy of the Nixon administration. Indeed, I have been informed this is so.

"Let me sum up the Middle East situation as I believe it is and has been. Israel, outnumbered one hundred to one in the population of unfriendly surrounding nations, has held its own with the help of American military supplies. In addition, the United States presence in the area has kept the Soviet Union outside the Middle East, at least as an active participant. If ever the United States gave up that role, it wouldn't make much difference whether or not we supplied arms to Israel.

"Since the ceasefire, the president has enlarged the role of the United States. He has moved boldly to befriend the Arab states and replaced the Soviet influence in those countries. I think the reaction of the Arabs has made it plain they were uncomfortable in their relations with Russia. This move puts the United States in a position of being able to influence the Arabs and act as an intermediary and a friend of both sides. Frankly, I believe it has been a brilliant policy, brilliantly carried out."

After Taiwan, the Republic of China, was ousted from the United Nations, the governor wrote directly to President and Madame Chiang Kai-chek, whom the Reagans had visited earlier on a mission for President Nixon:

"Mrs. Reagan and I want you to know how deeply shocked and disappointed we were by the completely immoral action of the U.N. General Assembly.

"I have told the President of my displeasure at what can only be described as the moral bankruptcy of an organization now reduced to the level of a kangaroo court."

The Captain of a Family

IT'S BEEN SAID that nobody really knows Ronald Reagan. While he is an open, warm, and thoughtful individual, he is also an intensely private man. I suspect that his being in the public eye almost from the time he was graduated from college has something to do with his trying to preserve what little privacy he can. But the air of dignity he lent to his office was certainly a factor in imparting that feeling of aloofness. He was always the governor; never one of the boys. A Ronald Reagan in a smoke-filled rap session after hours with his staff, or political friends, sitting behind the desk with rolled up shirt sleeves, open collar, feet on his desk, is as inconceivable to me as is the possibility that he might ever have been engaged in political shenanigans and intrigue. Of course he inherited an Irish temper and I must admit to having caught him using four-letter words. While they are in the mild category and wouldn't shock most people, he will blush and utter an embarrassed apology on catching himself.

It's been sheer pleasure to work for him, but it's my turn to be embarrassed when asked by my friends about what type of a man he is. When I tell the truth—which I feel I must—I sound like a propaganda agent, for who today believes there is a public servant among us who is everything we can ever hope to find: honest, dedicated, concerned, possessing both wisdom and foresight. Yet he truly has these qualities.

Home, with his wife and family, is the governor's favorite place. That's where he is happiest and relaxes the best. He adores and admires Nancy, his wife, and is a good friend and father to his children. The letters included in this section reveal much about Ronald Reagan's relationship with his family. They will tell you more about him than any story I might relate.

Lately, much has been said about political couples; the strains of office invariably take their toll. But Ronald and Nancy Reagan are a shining exception. They have shown that no occupation must automatically be a threat to a husband-wife relationship if there is sufficient love and understanding. It cannot be easy on any wife having to share her husband with twenty-one million constituents, but I'm certain Nancy Reagan never felt neglected, because he never allowed business to push her to the background. At the time, she fully understood her husband's responsibilities and took a great interest in what he was doing. Although she was careful never to interfere with his official duties, she was—and is—not afraid to speak her mind if she felt the staff pushed the governor too hard. The Reagans are totally devoted to each other. They have shared all the triumphs and defeats of his political career.

The governor has never been embarrassed about showing or writing about his love for Nancy. In a letter to Gregory C. Kimberlin, head of a Los Angeles community health center, he wrote: "I hope you all know how very sorry I am that I can't be with you today. Would you please tell your guest of honor that I will be calling on her when I get back to California, at which time I'll express my heartfelt appreciation for the effort she has put forth in this worthy cause as well as others.

"I have long admired her and upon my return to California intend not only to tell her that, but also that I love her more than anyone in the whole wide world."

It is only as the letter ends that you realize he is talking about Nancy. That was in 1974.

But in 1971 he received a request from Helen Gurley

Brown, editor of *Cosmopolitan,* asking him to jot down "the nicest thing a girl ever did for me."

The governor responded: "The nicest thing a girl ever did for me was when a girl named Nancy married me and brought a warmth and joy to my life that has grown with each passing year."

His sense of humor, which he often has to fight to keep from showing, came through in this letter, however, and he continued: "I know she won't mind if I say the second nicest thing was a letter from a little fifth grade girl last week. She added a P.S., 'You devil you.' I've walked with a swagger ever since."

The governor's children also have occupied an important place in his life. They were among the reasons the Reagans refused to live in the old governor's mansion when they first went to Sacramento. Not only was the house a firetrap but there was no place for the younger children to play and no neighboring homes which would provide playmates for the children.

When his son, Michael Reagan, was getting married the governor sent him a letter that expressed his own belief in the sacredness of the marriage vows:

"Dear Mike:

"Enclosed is the item I mentioned (with which goes a torn up IOU). I could stop here but I won't.

"You've heard all the jokes [that have] been rousted around by all the 'unhappy marrieds' and cynics. Now, in case no one has suggested it, there is another viewpoint. You have entered into the most meaningful relationship there is in all human life. It can be whatever you decide to make it.

"Some men feel their masculinity can only be proven if they play out in their own life all the locker-room stories, smugly confident that what a wife doesn't know won't hurt her. The truth is, somehow, way down inside, without her ever finding lipstick on the collar or catching a man in the flimsy excuse of where he was till 3 A.M., a wife does know, and with that knowing, some of the magic of this relationship disappears. There are more men griping about marriage who kicked the whole thing away themselves than there can ever be wives deserving of blame. There is an old law of physics that you can only get out of a thing as much as you put in. The man who puts into the marriage only half of what he owns will get that much out. Sure, there will be moments when you will see someone or think back on an earlier time when you will be challenged to see if you can still make the grade, but let me tell you how really great is the challenge of proving your masculinity and charm with one woman for the rest of your life. Any man can find a twerp here and there who will go along with cheating and it doesn't take all that much manhood. It does take quite a man to remain attractive and be loved by a woman who has heard him snore, seen him unshaven, tended him while he was sick, and washed his dirty underwear. Do that and keep her still feeling a warm glow and you will know some very beautiful music. If you truly love a girl, you shouldn't ever want her to feel, when she sees you greet a secretary or a girl you both know, that humiliation of wondering if she was someone who caused you to be late coming home, nor should you want any other woman to be able to meet your wife and know she was smiling behind her eyes as she looked at her, the woman you love, remembering this was the woman you rejected even momentarily for her favors.

"Mike, you know better than many what an unhappy home is and what it can do to others. Now you have a chance to make it come out the way it should. There is no greater happiness for a man than approaching a door at the end of a day knowing someone on the other side of that door is waiting for the sound of his footsteps.

"Love, Dad

"P.S. You'll never get in trouble if you say 'I love you' at least once a day."

The governor's younger son is named Ronald, also, but he is not a junior because he does not have his dad's middle name, Wilson. The Reagans nicknamed him "the Skipper." In late 1969 the governor took him to see the Los Angeles Rams professional football team play in the Los Angeles Coliseum. Following the game, he took Skipper to the dressing room to meet the Rams players. Afterward the following exchange of correspondence took place.

"Dear Governor Reagan:

"It was nice to see you after the game Sunday even if the occasion wasn't a happy one.

"I hope that Skipper got a few autographs and that he enjoys the game football.

"With all good wishes.

"Most sincerely,

"George Allen

"P.S. I'm checking on pads and helmet for Skipper and will send."

"Dear George:

"I had intended to write you but now can write and answer your kind letter. I'm most grateful to you for your help on the pads and helmet and want you to understand I didn't mean to be a freeloader on this. So please send a bill for whatever you are able to do.

"Now let me tell you about what that Sunday afternoon and the visit to the dressing room meant. This was our first chance to see the team other than by way of TV. We are all fans and the Skipper, I think, lives and dies with the Rams. He was, of course, greatly disappointed by the outcome of the game. You and I know, however, that defeats must be borne with the victories. But in the stands around us were those few to be found in any crowd—the fellows who wanted to talk about their beliefs that the pros shaved points to benefit the gamblers. Then there were other voices raised about, 'Well, they don't need this game, so they are not really making an effort.' With all that cynicism, particularly among those who have never been on the field themselves, I just want you to know that I walked out of that dressing room with my feet off the ground. To stand there with an eleven-year-old boy when his heroes dropped to their knees in prayer was something I'll never forget and for which I will always be grateful.

"Nothing a father could tell his son would ever match the impact of that moment. In spite of my own playing days and the years later as a sports announcer, I must confess to my surprise at that moment. But, it was a happy and thrilling surprise.

"Again, as I say, I don't know whether the fellows will ever know what that meant. I hope you don't mind that I've been giving some circulation among our friends to this experience, and it's been a most effective Christmas story.

"We'll be watching on the 27th and, if the power of positive thinking exists, you'll have two extra men on the field—me and the Skipper.

"Please give my best to all the men on the team.

"Sincerely,

"Ronald Reagan

"P.S. As far as I am concerned, California has no finer representatives or better ambassadors than the Rams."

The governor also wrote to the Rams' quarterback, Roman Gabriel, saying, in part, "I just wanted you to know how much I appreciate your kindness to him in the dressing room, but more than that, how very much the entire afternoon meant to me as a father. I'm referring to the impact on an eleven-year-old when he saw his heroes on their knees in prayer. I don't think any words of mine or any lecturing could ever match what this meant and the effect it had on him. And I couldn't begin to express what it meant to me to have him share that experience."

The governor also had occasion to write to the Skipper while he was attending Webb School in Claremont, California. Many a father has had the opportunity, or rather the responsibility, of writing this kind of letter to his own son:

"Dear Son:

"This letter may ramble a bit because it has to do with some concerns of mine. I suppose they are concerns every father has as he watches his son go through each year and period of life that he himself went through and remembers so much more clearly than you might think the opportunities he missed and the needless mistakes he made.

"Some fathers get so uptight in their concern they wind up trying to relive their own youth by stage-directing their son's life. I hope by now I've convinced you this is not my intention or desire. Some fathers cop out and, under the pretense of being a 'pal,' don't set any ground rules at all, and thus avoid having to make any tough decisions. This I have no intention of doing.

"These concerns have been on my mind for some time, and so has this letter. Now it has been triggered by your report card. You did fine in Ancient History—B+. You also had a B+ in English I, but an unsatisfactory effort. This makes the B+ less to be desired than a lower grade if the lower grade represented the absolute best effort of which you were capable. But then comes a lesser grade, a C— in French I, with a notation that, 'The quality of work has diminished quite a bit.' Again I say the C— would be all right with me if it represented your best try. This would be true also of the D in Algebra I, but the effort was rated unsatisfactory and the teacher's notation read, 'Ron has been relying on last year too long—he'd better force himself to get to work or he'll be in trouble.'

"Everything in life has a price and our biggest mistakes are when we don't really ask the price before we make our choice. Do you remember our Christmas shopping and the jolt you had when you had the gift wrapped and then heard the price?

"The 'trouble' the algebra teacher mentioned is the price you pay for not forcing yourself to work at something that is less interesting than other things you'd rather do. For example, the price can be ineligibility for outside activities, including athletics. It can be cancellation of summer plans because you have to make up credits in summer school. It can be limitation of your choice of colleges because you don't meet the requirements of the ones you'd really like. It can even be taking five years to get through school instead of four, and actually it can be all of these, which is quite a price to pay for a little goofing off.

"This period of the school year, whether it be high school or college, is the toughest. Don't ask me why, but it's always been true. This is when the excitement of fall and starting the new year seems a long way back and the summer an even longer way ahead. It's easy to get bored, to complain about everything and to think the school and everyone connected with it are out to ruin your life. This is when you have to remember the price for giving up and copping out. It's also the time when you build some character muscle to see you through real problems that come along later in life. And they do come along.

"It's only a few years now (they seem many to you) until you'll be out of school and really beginning your life. All that has gone before and these remaining few years of school and college are 'spring training' for the real season. When we are young we look at adults going about their day-to-day work and it all seems pretty dull and uninteresting. Believe me, that isn't so. I can't remember a time since graduation when I've been bored. Finding the thing you want to do and making a go of it is next in importance to finding the person you want to share your life with.

"Here again what you do now affects the choices you have. When I was announcing sports I was happy and thought that was all I wanted out of life. Then came the chance at Hollywood and that was even better. Now I'm doing something that makes everything else I've done seem dull as dishwater when I look back. But without some of the things I had to learn in college and didn't particularly care about, without some of the chores I didn't like when I was doing the G.E. television show, I couldn't do and wouldn't have had the chance to do what I'm doing now.

"We don't know what turns our life will take or what doors will open and there is nothing worse than to have such a door open and then learn you gave away your admittance ticket back in your school days.

"The other day when we were talking about the POWs we spoke of self-discipline and how it saved their lives. There is an inner man within all of us we have to call on once in a while. Having the guts to do the nasty little boring tasks, sticking to them when we'd rather goof off, decides whether that inner man has enough muscle to be of any help when we need him.

"Six months ago in the graduating class of the California Highway Patrol Academy there was a young man who led the class. He really wanted a career in the patrol, and being top man in that class took a lot of doing, both in the brain and the muscle departments. A couple of weeks ago on the

San Bernardino Freeway a drunk driver hit him and sheared his right leg off below the knee. Can you imagine what life looked like to him and his young wife? Oh sure, he'd get a pension, he wouldn't starve, but what would he do with his life besides sit on the front porch? Well, it won't be that way. He bought more than that with his willingness to put out at the academy. We are going to break the old rules and when he's up and on an artificial leg we are putting him back on duty as a patrolman. Now he has a double job—he has a chance if he makes it to open the door for others who suffer disabling injuries so they won't wind up in a rocker on the front porch. Think of the price he might be paying now if he'd decided to be just another kid 'getting by' when he was in the academy.

"Well, if you've read this far let me just wrap it up by telling you your mother and I have known many moments of great pride in you. We've also know moments of doubt in ourselves; times when we've worried as to whether we've made that inner man as strong as he'll need to be sometime later in life when you call on him for help.

"Keep an eye on the price tag; some things are very expensive and you pay for the rest of your life."

Governor Reagan, of course, wrote many letters to friends as well as to total strangers during his days in office. Once, for instance, he received a letter from a well-known actress and close friend who wrote that "my husband and I are house hunting. We love our present home, but we are literally being forced out of it by those darned 'movie-star maps.'

"Aside from having our doorbell rung at odd hours (once at 5 A.M., TRUE!), the cars line up in front of the house and people jump out and grab at the kids when they come home from school. Also, people in our profession are prime targets for robbers. Especially when it's announced we're out of town.

"So—we're moving. Still, I'm afraid that once we're settled in a new home, the same thing will start all over, after awhile. Maybe Arizona *is* the answer.

"I'm writing you because you, of all people, can certainly understand the problem.

"Is there *any* way of outlawing these maps and the people who sell them?

"I love my profession, and I love the public, but I *do* feel we are all entitled to the privacy of our home.

"Thank you for reading this, and any suggestions or leads you can give me will certainly be appreciated."

The governor replied:

"How I wish I could write a letter answering your problem. Unfortunately, there is no answer except the heartbreaking one you, yourselves, have found, which is to move. Evidently the law is such that records of addresses are open to public view and there is no way to prevent someone from pointing out a house and telling others who lives there. For what it's worth, let me tell you of my own experience some years ago.

"I discovered the buses were still stopping and identifying a house as mine from which I had long ago moved. It was then I learned that the houses must be within an area the buses can cover within a limited period of time. We had moved to the Palisades, and that was too far out for them, so they just kept on stopping at the same house. I don't know what your plans are or whether you have found a new home as yet, but it is something to think about. I believe Beverly Hills, Brentwood, and Bel Air, are probably the danger zones.

"Again, I wish I could ha sent a better and more satisfying answer. Nancy sends her best. We are still both watching and enjoying."

He also wrote to a total stranger—a newborn baby boy, the following:

"Dear Ronald:

"Welcome to the world. You'll probably have to ask who this other Ronald is by the time you can read this and the answer is, he's just someone who is highly honored that your parents chose his name for you.

"Some people will try to tell you this world you've come into is a pretty sick place. Don't you believe it. It's filled with wonderful people like your parents, and this country is the best part of that world so believe in it, serve it as best you can and love your fellow man.

"Sincerely,

"Ronald Reagan"

An emotional exchange of correspondence took place between the governor and the Reverend James E. Jones, pastor of Westminster Presbyterian Church in Los Angeles. The governor's reply again shows his reliance on the Lord.

The Reverend Jones wrote:

"Dear Mr. Reagan,

"In the spring of 1969 as president of the Los Angeles Unified School District I led a delegation of teachers up to Sacramento to discuss with you surplus dollars for schools and the cost of living and not tax refunds. Our request to see you was denied. Other controversial school matters produced in me great annoyance and resentment towards you as a person. Further, I even blamed you for my defeat in April 1969 when really the Lord knew my task on that board was finished. It was during the roasting of Bob Hope that God showed me my error, for you were having a great time that evening being truly 'human.' Then the night you gave your testimony at Coronado for the Laymen's Leadership Institute I knew that if I was to be really free I had to ask that you find it in your heart to forgive me. Strange that such a thing should stay on my heart, but this is the way the Spirit works. I trust that you will forgive the error of my way. I told Don Moomaw that such was so. Wherever you go, whatever you do rest assured that my blessings and prayers go with you."

And the governor replied:

"Dear Reverend Jones:

"From the bottom of my heart I thank you for your letter. There are no words to express what it means to me.

"In these past several years when frustrations built up it was very easy to be filled with bitterness and resentment amounting almost to hate. I don't know when the realization came to me of how inconsistent it was to ask God's help at the same time I was hating my brothers—his children.

"My most frequent prayer now is for forgiveness and help in conquering anger and bitterness. Oh, I can't claim total success but I'm trying. Your letter will make it much easier for me and for that I thank you."

The Ogre in Sacramento

ACTUALLY, IT IS this chapter which prompted me to want to publish the Reagan letters in the first place. Few men are as compassionate and as inherently kindly as the governor. That only a relatively few people seem to be aware of these traits can be blamed on his relentless opposition—those professional politicians and do-gooders—who see his fiscal responsibility and the courage he exhibited in cracking down on criminals and welfare chiselers as heartlessness towards the poor, the sick, and the old.

How very unfair!

Admittedly, of course, Ronald Reagan is not the only victim of such oratory. It's a stigma the liberals incessantly and successfully attach to conservatives, while claiming for themselves a monopoly of "concern for the little people." But since when can a man's feeling toward his fellow man be judged by his political or governmental philosophy?

Just because the governor demanded accountability from all government programs, including such sacred institutions as the University of California and the mental health program, just because he felt certain areas are better handled by the private sector, must this mean he doesn't identify with the people's desires and dreams and hopes, and doesn't care about their health, their education, and their welfare?

It's a convenient, demagogic accusation which, unfortunately, has created the myth that the Republicans in general and the governor in particular are insensitive to the people's needs and desires.

Having observed at firsthand for eight years one of these "cold, out-for-the-rich" Republicans, I find the situation ironic, to say the least. I am convinced that it would be impossible for any person with matching responsibilities to become more involved and be more sympathetic to individual hardship cases than was Governor Reagan.

Unfortunately, the best examples are not confined to one or two letters for easy publication in this chapter. There is no way in which I could adequately describe his interest in the well-being of two women, both in their fifties, who live on the meager state's contribution to their brother—a cerebral palsy victim. While it is true that their plight is self-imposed because they sternly refuse to commit "Buzzy" to the institution in which he rightfully belongs, the governor has never questioned their decision to honor their mother's deathbed request to personally take care of their unfortunate brother. The governor was genuinely touched when he received a letter from them a couple of years ago in which they told their sad story—that they couldn't get enough home work to sustain themselves even though they are skilled leather craftsmen and experienced writers, willing and able to take on any size order or work. What prompted them to write the governor was an administrative technicality which caused the loss of an increase in their brother's income on which they had counted to finally fill Buzzy's greatest wish: a rocking chair. Although the governor could not change state regulations and grant the increase, he so sympathized with their situation that he sent his own rocking chair. When he brought it into the office for shipping, our "don't you use it yourself" intervention brought a simple, "yeah, but this poor guy needs it more than I."

That was the beginning of a correspondence which expanded into an exchange of about a hundred letters in three years. What do they have to tell each other? Well, this unlikely relationship has developed out of a sense of sponsorship on the governor's part toward those three lonely people who are almost completely cut off from society and whose only complaint—despite severe hardships—has been a lack of opportunity to work.

The governor has been determined to do what he can to help them—so far with only limited success. But the fact that he tried and never gave up had a heartwarming and lasting effect on our whole staff. Here was the governor of the most populous state in the union, faced with a multitude of problems and pressures, talking to friends and visiting quality leathergoods stores in Beverly Hills like a traveling salesman, showing off Bertha and Sam's really magnificent craftsmanship and soliciting orders. At the same time, he personally wrote a number of small-town papers that he thought might be interested in starting a daily column with the sisters' folksy, but perceptive wisdom and humor.

Their several published books on California's colorful heritage have also been submitted to a movie producer. The governor is an eternal optimist and believer in our country's system and people. He knows that somehow, sometime, this family will find financial security, thus justifying his faith in our country's heritage of opportunity for all who are willing to work for it.

In late 1974 the sisters made a leather belt for former President Nixon and asked the governor to send it to him. Along with the belt went a note from the governor which said:

"Let me explain a little about this gift from 'Miss Sam and Miss Bertha.' I have never met them, but we have had a steady correspondence for about two years now. It all started with a problem they had regarding a state grant which is apparently their principal means of support.

"They have a 43-year-old younger brother who is mentally retarded and in their care. They promised their dying mother they would take care of him. He is mentally about three or four years old—plays with a teddy bear, etc. I was able to resolve their problem and also sent them a rocking chair they said 'Buzzy' (the brother) wanted for Christmas.

"They are an amazing pair. Nancy and I have received gifts since that time of their leather work, and they truly are masters of the ancient Spanish art of leather engraving.

I've shown their work to some specialty shops in the hope the gals could add to their income. Their work is so unusual that belts such as yours go for about $150."

Ronald Reagan's genuine concern for his less fortunate constituents developed into a regular sideline occupation for us. He made me responsible for making sure people who turn to him as a last resort were not turned away with a form letter, but rather brought to his attention. Then, somehow, whether it was through the state or his personal friends, he tried to be of help.

A very dear story involved a spunky nine-year-old Palm Desert boy who was very angry because he believed that the governor had cut his mother's welfare check just before Christmas. "Don't you know," he said in his letter to the governor, "that I don't have a father and my mother is disabled?" The governor, knowing that he had increased grants to the truly needy by tightening welfare eligibility standards, asked for an investigation. It was quickly determined that the boy was right—due to a clerical error his mother's income was inadvertently reduced.

Rather than merely settling for correcting the situation, he kept the family in mind and at the appropriate occasion asked Frank Sinatra, who resided near the boy, if he wouldn't like to play Santa Claus to this obviously deserving family. Sure enough, the response was "have beard, will travel." And Frank Sinatra, disguised with dark glasses, paid a personal call on this family, making sure he knew exactly the boy's great dreams and hopes. From the letters we subsequently received from both the boy and the mother, it was obvious that Frank Sinatra's legendary generosity provided for them a Christmas they will never forget.

In responding to the boy's first letter the governor hinted just a bit at what he had in mind. He wrote:

"I am truly sorry, Paul, about all the hardships you and your mother have had to endure. With regard to the welfare cutbacks you mentioned, you probably were notified by now that the Department of Social Welfare has made a mistake. I trust that's all straightened out now.

"Your mother must be very proud of you, Paul. I have heard from several sources what a fine young man you are, and that is a continuing source of happiness to any parent. It also makes up, I am sure, for many of the things your mother has to go without now. I hope you will remain such a serious, good student—it is the best start to a bright and happy future.

"Don't lose your faith in Santa Claus. I have a hunch he won't forget you."

After Christmas, the governor replied thusly to a letter of thanks from the boy's mother: "I enjoyed hearing from you, and please tell Paul I appreciated getting his nice letter.

"Let me tell you there were Santa's helpers and they really are the ones who deserve the credit. The matter of correcting the mistake about your check was handled by the good people in my office. The Santa of the bike and other things was Mr. Sinatra, who was happy to have had a part.

"I've relayed your letter to all concerned, and they all say Happy New Year."

There was a time when the governor literally gave the clothes off of his back to a constituent who wrote to him, "Will you please do me a little favor? I plan on getting married in about three months and I have been thinking maybe you would be kind enough to give me one of your used suits. I am very short of money now and I need a suit very badly. If you will do me this little favor I will thank you a million times."

Sure enough, the governor sent him a suit. And a letter came back: "Your beautiful suit came to me a few days ago and I wish to thank you a million times, it was a perfect fit and exactly my size."

In the letter the constituent disclosed his age. He was 80.

Once the governor received a letter from a soldier in Vietnam. It read: "In an attempt to find a dramatic way to show my wife how much I love her I would like to make what may be an unusual request of you—for you to deliver to her in person one dozen roses."

He hit the governor in a real soft spot. The governor wrote back that "I hope . . . I can, in this small way, show you my personal appreciation for the sacrifices all of you are bringing overseas for the rest of us."

And one night Ronald Reagan delivered a dozen red roses to the soldier's wife with the words, "Hello. I'm Ronald Reagan. Your husband asked me to deliver these flowers to you and tell you that he loves you."

The governor's soft spot for GIs overseas came through again when, on a visit to Vietnam, a young man who flew him in a helicopter handed him a note asking, "Could you please tell my parents that I'm all right?"

On his return home Governor Reagan wrote: "Nancy called your mother on our first day home. They had a nice visit and, I'm sure, a good cry together. Your mother is looking forward to your Christmas homecoming. She also told of your work with regard to the drug problem. May I just say a thank-you on behalf of all of us for that as well as what you are all doing in our behalf."

The governor was one of those who wore a POW/MIA bracelet with the name of missing in action Marine Captain Stephen Hanson. In 1973, when it was discovered that the man had been killed in action, the governor wrote to his widow, Carole, "I know there are no words that can be helpful at a time like this. Nancy and I feel so deeply sorry, and yet we know, too, there is a mercy in knowing definitely as you now know.

"This noon Nancy dedicated a display case in the corridor of the capitol, which will be a memorial to all of the men who were prisoners and missing in action. She placed the bracelet I have been wearing in the case. I've worn it so long I feel as though I had a personal knowledge and friendship with Steve. For some strange reason I have a feeling without the bracelet on that I, too, shall miss him. I know Todd must be quite a big boy now. Much different than that little fellow that tugged at my coat such a long time ago. None of us know the why of God's plan for us, but surely part of Steve's sacrifice must be validated by the pride that Todd is going to be able to have in his father. I'm sure Steve would say now to you and Todd, 'The world is for the living,' and if his sacrifice is to mean anything you must find happiness to make it all worthwhile.

"Nancy and I send you our warmest regards, our sympathy, and affection."

Tragic occurrences also brought letters from the governor. In one case a man collapsed and died while waiting to greet his son who was arriving home from a North Vietnamese prison camp. He wrote to the widow: "I have learned of your tragic loss just at the moment of happiness when your son returned from captivity. I wish there were words that could ease your burden of grief, but of course there are none.

"Your mind must dwell on the fact that your husband was denied seeing his son return. Please don't think me presumptuous, but as a father he already had the joy of knowing his son was alive and well. If our belief in God assures us of anything, it is that he did indeed see his son's return.

"Some years ago in a little town in the Midwest, the father of the star player on the high school football team died the day before the season's big game. No one, of course, expected his son to play. The coach told him he shouldn't feel as if he had to play, but the boy told him he wanted to. That afternoon he played the best game of his entire career. When the game was over he told the coach this was the first game his father had ever been able to see him play. His father had been blind all his life.

"Whatever God's plan is for each of us, we can only trust in His wisdom and mercy. Forgive me for invading your privacy at this time and please accept my deepest sympathy."

The cancer death of a dear friend's son brought this letter:

"I do know that your faith will serve you now; your belief that God does have a plan of infinite wisdom and mercy. It isn't given to us to understand at moments like this, we can only believe and trust in His goodness. Time will bring its healing, the pain will be less sharp, and you'll have memories that will grow warmer with the years. But those of us who care for you can only stand by, share some measure of your sorrow, and pray for that healing to come."

And the death of a slain policeman brought this letter:

"Words when you want and need them most seem very futile. Certainly I can find none to express my sympathy for you and my sense of personal loss and sorrow over the tragedy that has struck you and your family. I knew your husband in the kind of peculiar way that modern times have created between men of your husband's profession and those of us who are in public office.

"On a number of occasions he was one of those who provided security for me when I was in the area. It is true that such contact is only in passing with few opportunities for discussion or getting acquainted. Nevertheless, something else takes its place, at least as far as the protected is concerned. There is no way for me to describe the personal sense of gratitude and the real warmth I feel toward men like your husband who appear and are prepared to endure any risk to protect someone they have only just met. I am thankful we can still find such men in our land; without them, civilization itself would fail.

"I know your tragic loss must seem so senseless and without any rational explanation, but I have always believed that everything happens for a reason and that we must have faith in God's plan for all of us. It isn't given to us to understand—we can only have faith."

To a member of the Secret Service who lost a leg to cancer he wrote:

"I hope you won't mind my addressing you by your first name, but I've heard so much about you from Ed Hickey and some of the other fellows I know in the service that I just didn't feel I could be completely formal.

"They have told me of your operation, and I'm sure you must have some low moments when you wonder about the why of things. I don't know that I have any particular answers to questions of that kind, and yet from the vantage point of thirty-one years farther on, I have discovered that I believe very deeply in something I was raised to believe in by my mother. I now seem to have her faith that there is a divine plan, and that while we may not be able to see the reason for something at the time, things do happen for a reason and for the best. One day what has seemed to be an unbearable blow is revealed as having marked a turning point or a start leading to something worthwhile.

"From what Ed has told me, I know you need no words

of encouragement about facing this. You have within you all the courage you need. Forgive me for sticking my nose in, but it's a privilege a fellow insists upon after he's gotten those other thirty-one years."

A Time for Planting

IF THE GOVERNOR has one really soft spot in his heart, it's for children and young people. I can't recall the number of times all other business stopped or had to wait because he became involved with a group of youngsters having more questions than the governor had time on our calendar.

"Our biggest investment in the future is our kids," he gently explained to anyone who tried to hurry him when he was engaged in conversation with either one or a whole class of students, "and there is no time better spent."

A widely hailed program instituted during his administration was a show called "Young People's TV." It was coordinated through the State Department of Education which selected at random groups of high school students to meet with the governor in question and answer sessions twice a month. These shows were videotaped for later airing on campuses and on cable television.

It wasn't just the students who benefited from this exchange of ideas. The governor freely admitted that these get-togethers were valuable to him. That he enjoyed them was obvious. Many times the end of the taping wasn't the end of the discussion, for he would invite the students into his office for more talk.

I used to marvel at the patience he showed on many such occasions. A few students came from conservative families and felt honored at the chance to meet their governor. Many came from low-income neighborhoods and couldn't wait to point aggressive, if not hostile, questions toward the governor. Some didn't try to conceal their prejudice and antagonism.

Nevertheless, the governor never reacted in kind. Instead he tried with a zeal rarely found in teachers to reshape and broaden their thinking. What often made it difficult for him was the students' basic ignorance about their government, the economy, and history. But his efforts were generally rewarded as students who came with chips on their shoulders often left feeling the governor had dealt honestly and understandingly with them.

His disappointments—and there were some—came not when students continued to disagree with him but when once in a while they refused to acknowledge his sincerity or to give him credit for doing what he thought was right.

Perhaps I should not start out a chapter on a bad note, but there was one group of high-school girls whose churlish attitudes were reflected both in their first letters and in their replies to his letter. It was difficult for the governor to understand the rudeness and belligerence of these girls, and he did not bother to respond to their second letters.

When the girls' first letters were called to the governor's attention he was appalled, not only at their ignorance, but also at the accusatory tone and antagonism in each. As a result, he wrote to the principal of the school saying that "I conclude that writing the letters to me was a class project. This is certainly the way responsible citizens should communicate their thoughts and questions to their elected leaders. . . . However, I am appalled at what else is being taught —or not taught—in this instance."

He pointed out that as the recipient of up to 10,000 letters a week he could not answer all of his mail personally, as the girls demanded. He added, however, that "I can and do choose those which merit personal attention. Normally I would say these do not, but I intend to answer each one of them if for no other reason than perhaps my letter will give them a better perspective than they have been given in the classroom. The spelling and grammatical errors in these letters, incidentally, are extremely interesting for a government class in high school. Especially so the misuse or misspelling of the word 'capitol'.

"The next time this teacher asks his or her students to write to a public official I believe he (she) would be well advised to stop and reflect: What will their letters reveal about what, and how, I have taught them?"

Each girl was sent a copy of that letter along with an individual response. The fact that the governor replied to them pleased them not at all. The fact that he wrote to their principal incensed them.

The girls' initial letters contained such sentences and phrases as:

"Just because you've got more money than a lot of people doesn't mean that you should completely ignore the subject (of the Homestead Act)."

"You won't get any votes out of me in the next election unless you get with it."

"I think you guys are just too lazy or are too busy with other things, like trying to raise income tax."

"I hate what you are doing. Either sitting in your office on some throne or in a private jet somewhere. We voted you in last time and now are voting you out."

"I have had it with the school system and it is worthless to me."

"By the time your [sic] up for election again I'll be abe [sic] to vote for you, but I wont [sic]!"

"With the way your [sic] going you wont [sic] get a damb [sic] vote out of me."

"The rate that things are going now, I hope you lose!!!"

"P.S. Start trying to improve or get out! Shape up! or ship up! [sic] I can really hurt you? [sic] Watch out in 74!"

One of the governor's replies will suffice.

"I don't know what grade you received in your high school class for writing your letter to me, but I'm afraid I have to give you a rather low grade on your understanding of government and which branch of government is in charge of things like the Homestead Act. The governor of a state can do nothing about changing the Homestead Act, since that is a matter of the federal government in Washington.

If, however, you were referring to regulations limiting the value of property to be homesteaded under state law, I think you should know that you are completely wrong about the values you listed. The $12,500 limitation hasn't been in effect since 1963. In that year it was raised to $15,000, but last year (1971) I signed legislation increasing it to $20,000. You will note I said I *signed* legislation. This is not a matter that a governor can simply rule on; the legislature must introduce a bill and pass it by a majority vote in both houses. Then the governor has the right to either sign or veto.

"As for not getting any votes from you in the next election, I'm surprised that you haven't been told that when my term ends in 1974 I have stated publicly and repeatedly that I am not running for re-election.

"Now let's take up your point about pollution and how horrible the world is becoming. California's air-quality standards are the highest in the nation. In fact, we had to get special permission from Washington because our laws are more strict than the national laws. The same is also true of water pollution, and we have a program at work in California aimed at further cleaning our waters and certainly eliminating as much of air pollution as is possible. The truth is, while you perhaps don't recognize it on a smoggy day, we have made gains. The air is actually getting cleaner, but it will be of course a few years before it will become apparent. After all, we only discovered what causes smog a few years ago, and the scientist who made that discovery is employed by the state to try and find the answers to it.

"Now you speak of littering. Yes, it's true we have signs posted, and we hope that citizens who see someone violating the law will take license numbers and report these citizens to us. It must be obvious to you that our highway patrolmen can't be every place at every moment when someone throws refuse out of a car window. But isn't this a problem that really finds the people at fault? Government doesn't litter the roadside or throw garbage in the river—people do—and the task is for people like yourself to spread the word until the vast majority of our people are as law-abiding in this as they are with regard to any other crime, such as stealing or murder.

"Then you say that I am either too lazy or too busy with other things like trying to raise income taxes. Again, you are hopelessly misinformed. I have just made a public announcement asking for a reduction of the income tax and promising if the legislature will not act, to allow the people to vote themselves a ten percent cut in the income tax. For four years I have tried to get tax reform that would reduce the homeowner's property tax. I have been balked by a small band of legislators who have refused to give the needed votes to pass this program.

"A great many people are saying things and writing things expressing views on public affairs. You will be better off if you realize there is usually more than one view on any such issue. Make sure you do not just accept one person's viewpoint. Find out for yourself what is the other side of an issue. The only way our system of government will work is with a well-informed citizenry—people who cannot be fooled by a column in a paper or a statement in a classroom, but will insist in finding out the truth of the matter for themselves."

The girls completely misread the governor's courteous gesture in sending them copies of his letter to the principal. Those who responded to him wrote in this vein:

"Now I would like to discuss why you sent these letters we wrote to *you*, were sent to Mr. Glaze with a letter, of which I received a copy. In *my* opinion you sent these letters back to our principal because you wanted to show us that our place in this world is sitting in our classes and keeping quiet. Well I am sorry, that is not how I intend to spend the rest of my life, sitting in some little corner and being quiet. If I think something is wrong I intend to let it be known, one way or another. If your intentions was [sic] to get any of us, including our teacher, into any trouble, then at least in my case there will be a fight. Maybe your intentions were to treat us like children by reporting us to our principal, instead I think you should be talking to us as young adults. Reporting us to our principal was a very childish thing to do."

The governor felt these second letters were best unanswered.

But these kinds of letters were rare. In contrast was a series of letters he exchanged over a period of two years with a high-school girl in his old home town of Dixon, Illinois. Her name was Petra Rusev. She was fourteen and a freshman when the correspondence began.

Petra began the correspondence with a cry for help. The Dixon high-school stage was condemned, the lights were bad, there would probably be no more plays, no more musicals on the stage where Ronald Reagan first began acting. Petra was determined to start a fund-raising drive to make it possible for the shows to go on.

"Please, Governor Ragan" [sic] she wrote, "would you help us out with a donation? I know this is a lot to ask of you but you see, you have a lot going for you and are famous. Can you help some of us get something going before all is lost?

"Nobody in the whole world knows that I wrote this letter because I want it that way. The only person's hopes that are high right now are mine. I love my school and want to do something for it. You probably did too when you went to DHS. I want to say too that if you help us there will be something nice to repay you for what you've done. Please! Please! Please! Try and help your old Alma Mater out.

"Please try and answer soon and also understand that I will be overjoyed if you can help, but I will also understand if you can't. Think about it! Please! Thank you for your time.

"Bless you,

"Sincerely,

"Petra Rusev"

Petra was a new name to the governor. He wrote back to Mr. Petra Rusev:

"I remember everything about the plays I did in Dixon High and certainly know how you feel. I also understand those people who voted against a possible increase in their taxes. Sometimes hard decisions have to be made by grown-ups, and they are not always happy with what they have to do.

"Before I get back to your problem with the 'stage,' let

me just point out some of the problems the people in Dixon, and in most of the rest of the country, have. Right now in California, taxes (federal, state, and local) take forty-three cents of every dollar the people can earn. The figure in Illinois is the same or very close to that. Now this means the average person works from New Year's until the first week in June just to pay taxes. Government is the biggest expense a citizen has. It costs more than food, clothing, and housing for a man's entire family. I point this out only so you won't have any bitterness about what the people of Dixon did.

"Now, about the stage and the plays you want to put on. Believe me, I agree that is a very wonderful part of your high-school experience. I'll restrain myself from any 'what things were like' stories about D.H.S. in my day. I don't know what other facilities there may be in Dixon now that might be used temporarily. That is something you'd know better than I and something you might want to check on.

"Then there is another possibility—fund-raising—to get the money to repair the stage and make it safe. You've already thought of that as your letter indicates. This is really a possibility and you might be surprised at how many people would help once they knew the students were willing to work themselves to make it happen.

"Just yesterday, a glee club from a small college (250 students) in 'Pippa Passes,' Kentucky, sang here at the capitol in California. Pippa Passes is just down the road from Possum Trot—word of honor! The glee club is on a two-month tour of the country and they earned and raised $20,000 to pay for the trip.

"I'm enclosing a check for $50. I wish it could be more. But, if you decide to try and raise the funds for the stage, use this as a first contribution and let me know how things work out."

Petra was thrilled as her return letter indicates. She signed it (Miss) Petra Rusev.

She also corrected her spelling of the governor's last name.

"Dear Governor Reagan," she wrote:

"How can I ever thank you for your kindness and

thoughtfulness. You can also be sure that I understand about the taxes too. Important decisions have to be made, and I guess they're just not the way you want them sometimes.

"I had quite a time keeping the good news in me when I received your letter and check. I was just tickled to death! I did tell one person besides my family though and that is a girl who is very much interested in acting also. She and I are going to work together to get this show on the road.

"Today Jenny and I went to talk to Mr. Wiltz, our choral director. You should have seen his mouth drop open. I think he lost his words all together. After we discussed it with him, we went and talked to Mr. Boyer, our principal.

"Mr. Boyer's reaction was the same. We had a long talk and this is what we decided. Jenny and I are going to appear before the board and present everything to them. After their approval (which I'm sure we'll get), we are going to start all kinds of fund-raising and your check is the first donation and the base of everything.

"The Dixon station is going to keep a day open for people to call in and pledge money. We are also planning to collect money in town, door-to-door, and at the next choral concert. That is the plan Jenny and I have made and I can't wait for suggestions from the other students. I just have to keep my fingers crossed that all goes well at the board meeting.

"Thank you! Thank you! Thank you! That is all I can say because I am *so* grateful. You can be sure that I will keep you posted on what happens. You really are a great man!"

On February 16, 1973, the governor responded:

"I can't tell you how happy I was to receive your letter and to hear of your plans. You have a great opportunity now to prove what the people can do on their own without always having to go through government channels and fund things out of taxes.

"You'll probably have many discouragements. Anyone who is trying to enlist aid and support for a good cause does, but keep after it. At the end of the road, I'm sure there can be success and all that you have hoped for.

"I would appreciate it very much if from time to time you would give me a progress report and let me know how you're doing. You didn't mention the newspaper. I hope it will be included in your plans because it can be a great help in letting people know of your undertaking.

"Best regards."

Petra and Jenny did indeed appear before the Board of Education and their appearance resulted in a story in the *Dixon Telegraph* headed "Reagan's check launches fund drive to remodel DHS auditorium." The story noted "the check from Reagan was not a rubber-stamped document, but handwritten on the governor's personal account."

The clipping, sent by Quincy Adams of Dixon, brought this letter from the governor:

"Just a line to thank you for sending me the story from the *Telegraph*. I didn't know there had been any public reaction to my correspondence with Petra Rusev so I enjoyed seeing the paper. Incidentally, from her letters she must be quite a nice young lady, and the Dixon schools are doing a good job it would seem."

Petra wrote him again on March 4.

"Dear Governor Reagan,

"Thank you so very much for your last letter which you sent to me. I get so excited when I receive a letter from you. I have a lot of good news to tell you.

"We had our midwinter choral concert last week. Mr. Wiltz told the people that we were taking donations for the auditorium fund and we would greatly appreciate it if they would give. The people were more than happy to give. We had a girl stationed at each exit and when the people were all gone, every box was full.

"We collected a total of $241.23. This was pretty good because there really weren't too many people there. Three clubs also gave us a check for $25 which come to $75. This, along with your check and the 60 marks my grandmother sent from Germany, now gives us a total of $386.23, which we think is pretty good for only collecting one time.

"We are in the process of forming a committee to arrange collection dates in town, door-to-door, and then people may also call in over WSDR, which is a radio station, and pledge money. Mr. Wiltz is pretty busy right now, because the tryouts for the musical are coming up. I'm going to see to it that the committee meets before tryouts because we want to get things going and not let them go to sleep.

"I'm sorry I forgot to tell you about the paper. It was truly a big help in publicizing the matter. I was pretty famous the day after the board meeting. I am enclosing the article that was in the paper about your check. I will also be happy to write you from time to time and tell you how things are going."

And again the governor replied:

"Dear Petra:

"This is the end of a long, busy day, so I'll just drop you a line to say how delighted I am to hear of your progress. I know you have a long way to go, but keep trying, get others involved, and above all don't get discouraged."

In mid-May there was a letter of discouragement from Petra. Nothing was going right. The adults were too busy with other things to show any interest. She was not allowed to seek donations at school events where admission was charged. "I'm so very mixed up that I just can't think straight anymore. I don't want to give up, but sometimes I feel as if it's the only logical thing to do. . . ."

In response, the governor wrote to his old friend, Ben T. Shaw, of the *Dixon Evening Telegraph*:

"Dear Ben:

"Maybe this should be a letter to the editor. Anyway, I have a problem, and I'm turning to you for help.

"Sometime ago I received a letter from a Dixon High School student, Petra Rusev, telling me of the need for repairs to the 'stage' the students use for their plays. She was upset with the failure of a bond issue to pass and reminded me of how important a play had been to me once on the Dixon High School stage.

"I didn't need that reminder because I still think that much of what has happened that is good in my life began in the old Northside High School when I first 'trod the boards' in Phillip Barry's play, *You and I*, under the direction of B. J. Frazier.

"In replying to her letter I suggested starting a fund-raising drive and told her she'd be surprised at how many people would help once they knew the students were willing to work themselves to make it happen. She took it from there and with great enthusiasm set out on that course. I know your paper gave a boost because she sent me the clipping, also the most recent photo of her receiving a check from Mrs. McLennan of the American Legion Auxiliary. (Petra and I have kept up a correspondence!)

"My problem is her most recent letter. She hasn't faltered in her effort to get help for what seems like a most worthy project. Now, however, she seems pretty much alone in the crusade. The apathy which you and I know so well has set in after an enthusiastic start. Oh, she is still trying, the apathy is on the part of others, and to a young lady her age the goal seems discouragingly distant.

"Ben, she's trying to do what you and I have believed in so long. She hasn't joined that ever-growing crowd who look to government as the giver of all good things. Her letters have been heartening accounts of progress and cheerful acceptance of setbacks. But it's been a long stretch and the term is ending. Can you really afford to let her and those other young people fail? It's almost like saying, 'Don't try—just wait for a government handout of some kind.'

"I know from her letters that many of the good people of Dixon have helped, but what of the others? Is there a way to arouse their interest? That's my problem, Ben. I know it's a long way from Sacramento, but I've never felt all that far from the Rock River—especially when summer's coming on."

Mr. Shaw reported back the following:

"Your letter of May 31st about the remodeling of the Dixon High School stage has been discussed with Arnold Lund, our general manager, and Robert Nellis, city editor. Two reporters, Leonard Ingrassia and Tom Shaw, my grandson, interviewed Miss Petra Rusev about the stage needs and problems of getting money to have the work done.

"Miss Rusev wants new lights, new curtains, cushions for audience seats and rehabilitation of rooms under the stage. She tackled these problems at a time when the principal and school board were very busy with students in the final period of the school year. These administrators will have a meeting in about two weeks and then plan the fund drive. We will send copies of the papers with news stories so you will know the results.

"Ronald, you have delighted this young girl with your thoughtfulness in encouraging her to work for this program. I think she is of Russian descent, and then her folks came from Germany. Her father is dead. Miss Petra Rusev is thrilled to know someone as busy as the governor of California would take the interest to send money from the request of a stranger. She shows your letters to everyone she talks with. I agree with her."

The governor sent a copy of his letter to Mr. Shaw to Petra. And in July she wrote:

"How can I ever thank you for your thoughtfulness! When I read your letter to Ben T. Shaw, it just made me cry. It made me realize how much you really care. I just wish all people were as considerate as you."

She went on to tell how the *Telegraph* was going to help with the project and how it had been decided "to kick off the new school year with the fund drive for the auditorium. We figured that this would be a chance where all the students would be back and wanting to do something together."

She concluded: "I want to thank you again for everything that you have done for me, to help me, and to help our auditorium. I just love you for it. You're really one of the greatest men that ever lived. Thanks to you I have hope again, and this time I know I'm not going to give up. Thank you! Thank you! Thank you!"

After school began Petra wrote again, describing her recruitment for the drama club, and the club's publicity and fund-raising efforts for the auditorium.

Before closing she wrote:

"I want to thank you so much for all the help you have given me. Several times I have felt like giving up, but your letters have always given me a lift, and the courage to go on. Thanks a million!!!"

The governor wrote back:

". . . you'll come to realize fund-raising is not easy. There are many worthwhile causes competing with each other for the money people have to contribute and it is drudgery and hard work, but you seem to be covering all bases. I don't know anything that I could suggest now beyond what you're doing, exploring every possibility. You might think in terms of cans with slitted tops through which people could insert money stating what they're for and seeing if merchants would permit them to be placed in their places of business so that people could drop a coin in on their way in or out. One other thing might be helpful; if either in the paper or in some public place in town, say at the main intersection, you could mount a kind of thermometer that would show each week the level of funding with the figure of the amount actually needed. To watch the thermometer climb might serve as a reminder to people and they may get the idea of wanting to help see the thermometer reach the goal. . . ."

By November 4, the fund drive had been held and Petra wrote that "we now have a total of $3895.68 but," she noted, "the lighting board costs approximately $13,000 and I have no idea how much the area under the stage costs. The roof also leaks and the coat of paint that is now on the auditorium walls is the original.

"I really hope that we use the money and put it to use soon, because I feel that the people want to see something done with it.

"I am envied by a great many people," she continued. "I also hope that we can still keep up a correspondence such as we have been doing. It makes me so happy to be able to write to you. . . . We here in Dixon all love you!!!"

The governor responded:

"Congratulations! You've done a fine thing. I'm sure you've learned a great many things too. You've found out that good things just don't happen; there have to be people willing to make an extra effort to cause them to happen. I hope you've also learned that people are basically good and want to help.

"It's been a long road from that first letter when you were so disappointed about the bond issue to the happy letter I've just read.

"Now, why don't you sit down with the school authorities and see what is the top-priority problem in the auditorium that can be solved with the money you've raised? All of us all our lives have to do that—even governments. There is always more that needs doing than we can afford at any one time so we do it step by step. You've proven it can be done, others will be encouraged by your example to take up the cause in the years ahead."

By Thanksgiving Petra had written that an anonymous donor had given $1,000 to the drive. "When Mr. Boyer the principal told me, I was so happy I started crying. Then the Lions Club gave $250, the FHA gave $100, FFA gave $25 and things are really looking bright. It's all thanks to you, Governor Reagan." She signed it "One of your many fans" and P.S.'d, "I hope you had a very nice Thanksgiving. You couldn't deserve it more."

And so the letters continued. Petra reported the fund up to $8,000 and that the school board decided to buy a new lighting board without tapping the fund. The governor responded to one letter, "Since your letters of late have only been filled with good and exciting news, they have become regular day-brighteners. Thanks for sharing all the wonderful things that have happened."

In the following October came further news: "The auditorium is absolutely beautiful! We have added so very much to it. The sound system is getting finished up. We have the complete new ventilation system. We have gold wall-to-wall carpeting and brand new gold curtains. The whole auditorium had been repainted in a beautiful gold and white. The new lighting board isn't completely installed, but it's getting there. You wouldn't believe the change, Governor Reagan."

She concluded: "I'd like to end by saying thank you again for all the help you have given me, and the many words of encouragement when I was so close to giving up. I'll never be able to repay you. We've come so far and still have a long way to go, but now I know we can do it. I have to go now, cause it's getting late. Take care and God bless you.

"Love, Petra."

The governor's letter of reply was a little nostalgic. "By

the time you receive this, a new governor will have been elected here. It's really hard to believe my term is at an end . . . your days sound busy and full of excitement. Take full advantage of these times. I know my school days bring back many good memories, and they seem to go much too fast."

That was the last of the letters while Ronald Reagan was governor. But the correspondence continues. I hope it goes on for as long as they both live.

Petra was unusual in that she became a regular correspondent with the governor. Most of the young people wrote only once or twice. Once in a while one would send along a little gift. Deborah Westrick of Fresno sent him "a doll I made of you. Inside is a story of your life. I think you're a very important man. I don't know what you look like but I tried my best to make you like you really are." The doll has black yarn for hair and eyebrows, and buttons for eyes. It has no ears. But inside is, indeed, a story of his life, beginning, "Ronald Reagan was a one-time motion picture star," and ending, "He is our present governor and has done a tremendous job."

A young man, whose parents were long-time friends of Ronald Reagan, wrote the governor that despite his affection and regard for him he felt the Republicans as a party lack compassion and therefore he had joined the Democratic party.

The governor, a Democrat himself most of his life, wrote a lengthy reply:

"I appreciate your letter and your motive in wanting to write me, but will not deny I am disappointed. You certainly have every right to choose your course, and my personal regard for you will be unaffected by your decision.

"We have a two-party system. It can only exist if people belong to each of those parties and the parties themselves stand for something. Now, however, at the risk of seeming to contradict myself, let me touch on the reasons you have given for your change.

"First, your commendable compassion for the black and the poor. I will take second to no one in my criticism of these past decades of so-called welfare. Not because of lack of compassion, but because those in charge were willing to create a class of people hopelessly mired forever in the swamp of permanent dole or handout. In our state, I am sure you are aware of the tremendous efforts we've made to break this pattern. What you can't know about is the frustration over these last two years of having a Washington bureaucracy throw obstacles in the way of our every effort to find a new method of helping. This, of course, touches on the racial issues as well.

"Do you know that the national average of black unemployment to white is 2½ to 1? Do you know, also, that in the great Los Angeles–Long Beach industrial area, we've reduced that ratio in these last two years to 1.4 to 1?

"Perhaps your feeling is due in part to the campus situation at San Francisco State where the issue has been successfully heralded as racial. There were approximately three hundred BSU [Black Student Union] members on strike. There have been and are about nine hundred black students going through the picket lines to attend classes. Many of them have taken beatings, threats to their lives, and vandalism to their cars and property. Whose side do I take?

"My administration has placed more Negroes and Americans of Mexican descent in executive and policy-making positions than any administration in the history of California. A number of these individuals have now been taken to Washington by the new administration. I'll grant you don't see many headline stories about this. Now, admittedly, I'm talking about California and my administration of more than two years. Shouldn't we keep in mind that Nixon has only been president two months? When I look back on my own first two months and realize how much more gigantic is his task of organizing an administration, I don't think it's possible to say at this point what direction he is taking, or what his policy will be. It's very difficult to speak critically of a victim of a tragic assassination, but I must point out that President Kennedy in two years hadn't succeeded in getting a single portion of his program through the Democratic Congress.

"You speak of the war and guns not being the answer,

but do we know whether secret negotiations to end the war are going on or not? Obviously, if they are, we can't know about them or they are no longer secret and no longer effective. Certain journalists are on rumor expeditions, fishing for hints as to whether something of the kind is going on. Let me just add some history. It was a Democratic president who first ordered American combat units into the fighting, and it was his attorney general who said this was necessary to erase from the Russian minds any idea of our weakness as a result of the Bay of Pigs. I think someone could question whether that was enough of a motive for a war.

"But now, let me get to the real item of greatest concern to me, and based on our last conversation, of concern to you, also: Your generation and the communication gap. The schools grow bigger; government and the establishment grow bigger; and the young begin to feel they are numbers on a computer card.

"Who created this establishment? Whose philosophy over the period of your lifetime has consistently urged more and more government?

"For more than twenty years I've traveled the mashed potato circuit arguing for less government and more individual freedom. Over that same period, I have been attacked as a reactionary because the prevailing philosophy has been that only big government can have the answers in this complex world. How do I go about communicating with your generation? I've had campus editors, student body presidents, and student groups here in the office. I correspond with students who have written to tell me they fear discrimination by teachers and administrators who favor those who would radicalize the campus. I'd like nothing better than to speak on the campus and have the kind of question and answer sessions we had during the campaign, but you know what would happen. The dissidents would make it impossible for me to communicate as they have with other speakers, cabinet members, and even the Vice President.

"The other night, I heard Humphrey on the Joey Bishop Show answering a question about campus disorders. I thought he described the dissidents as being two groups: a hard inner core of outright revolutionaries bent on destruction, surrounded by a larger group of misguided students who sincerely believe they are promoting a legitimate cause. There was more, but all of it was virtually word for word what I have been saying for quite some time. Yet, less than a year ago, this same Humphrey was holding me up to ridicule for saying exactly this.

"You say guns are not the answer on the campus. Of course not. But do you know of the hours I've spent in regents meetings and in conferences with university administrators begging them to take the firm action only they can take to solve these problems? When force must be sent to the campus, it is made necessary by their failure to use their own power, their own regulation to settle these issues. Then, faced with physical assault on other people, arson, bombing, destruction of property, the law must be called in. It is not true that the police escalated the action when the university finally asked me to declare a state of emergency at Berkeley. Wheeler Hall already had been burned down. Hundreds of thousands of dollars in damage had already been done. Students had been beaten by literally lynch mobs for simply trying to attend class.

"You speak of compassion—and, Steve, the announced causes of the campus disturbances are so often in the name of love for the downtrodden—but compassion is broader than just a theoretical concern about the disadvantaged. Twenty students caught a campus policeman alone and beat him and kicked him as he lay on the ground until he was hospitalized. Did they feel compassion? Did even one of them, for a second, look at his face there on the ground, wonder about him, wonder if perhaps a wife at home was preparing a meal for his homecoming? Wonder perhaps if he himself didn't have children, which incidentally he did, and whether they called him 'dad,' depended on him to help them with their homework and fix a broken toy?

"I have said over and over again that many of the announced causes of the campus disorder are worthwhile suggestions and could very easily be implemented. And I would favor implementing—but, Steve, the one issue that makes this impossible is when any group takes to the street and then with the threat of violence or coercion says 'Meet our demands, or we burn the place down, or prevent others from getting an education.' There can be no orderly society or respect for the rights of the individual if any administrative body or government body establishes the precedent of giving in to such a demand. This is like the first payment to a blackmailer. Once you embark on that path, what group, with what demand, might be outside next week?

"I listened for two hours while the university administration told me how terribly complex the campus problem was, how complicated it was to try and discipline those who were administering the beatings, breaking the windows, planting the bombs. Finally, I asked one question: 'How complex would it be if the mob outside was under the auspices of the Ku Klux Klan?' I have an uneasy feeling they would know how to handle this in about three and a half minutes. In short, I am charging that their own, so-called liberal philosophy, making them sympathetic to the announced aims of the riots, blinds them to their responsibility to offer protection to the others on the campus.

"Well, this has been a very long discourse, I know, and perhaps should take place in conversation, and not in writing. I suppose I am concerned, not about your right to choose a direction, but because your reasons for the change are not valid in the face of what seems to be the continuing big-government philosophy of the party you have chosen.

"Steve, in a few days I'll be meeting with the student body presidents of the campuses and yet, not one of them was elected by as much as ten percent of the student body. Is this a recommendation for lowering the voting age? Are we not justified in suggesting, first, that the student body in much larger numbers handle some of their own affairs, such as the election of student government which has in its hand the power to expend millions of dollars of compulsory dues? Could I suggest that perhaps the majority of the students start making their own views known about the violence and the disruptions on the campuses, instead of simply bypassing it as of no concern?

"And lastly, let me just say, I'll return to the Democratic party, too, if and when that party's philosophy recognizes once again the preeminence of the individual, the limitations of what government can accomplish, and the necessity for turning to the people themselves for help in solving the great social and human problems. . . .

"If I continue this letter another page and a half, it will have to be bound as a book, so I'd better quit here. One of these days, I hope we can have a talk."

Many young people wrote to ask him about his job as governor. To one he replied: "You ask how it feels to be governor and is the work hard? That is not as easy to answer as you might think. You know many hours of frustration as governor when things you think should be done are delayed or halted by petty politics, but you also know many days of great satisfaction and a sense of accomplishment." He ended: "This job is so challenging and so exciting that I haven't missed my other profession at all."

The letters from young people covered the broadest possible spectrum, as can be seen from the following excerpts:

A young man asked him what word he found most objectionable. His answer:

"As I thought more and more about your request I sat back and let my mind go as to just what word jolts me the most and, curiously enough, it turned out not to be one of those obscenities. I do not mind the use of profanity in a dramatic production or literature when it is appropriate, and I mean by this the usual words of 'hell' and 'damn,' etc. I find, however, that when God's name is invoked and tied to one of those words, it is very jarring. Profanity, as we all know, is a substitute for a lack of vocabulary, but the use of the name of God in connection with that is a violation of one of the commandments. I had not realized how strongly I felt about it until you asked your question.

"Strangely enough, in the old days of vaudeville, which was somewhat ribald, vaudeville comics would use the words 'damn,' 'hell' and others, but there was an unwritten rule of show business then; they never used the word 'God.' I wish we could return to that custom."

A young lady who was a Stanford University journalism student wrote him a complimentary letter. A pleased Governor Reagan wrote back that "you were very kind. . . . It might interest you to know that you are the first student of all the journalism classes I've met with who ever wrote such a letter. Please know that you brightened my day considerably."

He added, "If you'll forgive my rewarding you for your kindness with some unsolicited (and probably unnecessary) advice—search for the truth always; see if there is another side to every issue."

Another young lady asked him about the method of selecting presidents and vice presidents. ". . . we seem to have done pretty well with the system as it is," he responded, but continued: ". . . I have not, until now, given any serious thought to how the system could be changed. We might look at the position of the vice president, or candidates for that job, as men running for the presidency, going into primaries and soliciting the people's support. Having been chosen by the people in the primary, I would then suggest that the president and vice president run as a ticket as they do today to obviate the possibility of having a president of one party and a vice president of the other.

"If we were to go to a national primary as you suggest, and incidentally so many states are now having them we almost have a national today, we should be very careful to not change the voting system to where we have a president chosen by national popular vote. If this should come about, it might destroy once and for all our system of fifty sovereign states banded together into a federation.

". . . we should strengthen, rather than weaken our federated system. Few people realize what a great protection of freedom there is in the present system. The fact that anyone at any time can move across a state line is a protection against tyranny in state government. . . . For that reason, we should also be on guard against further centralization of authority in the nation's capital."

Many times answers to letters from young people found the governor stating and in a way renewing his own strong love for and faith in America and our system of government. He was not hesitant to point out errors we have made but the love always came through. This letter to Carrie S. Palmer is an example:

"Dear Carrie:

"Thank you for writing and for giving me a chance to express myself on the matters that concern you. You describe yourself as a 'common person' and again later refer to the 'common people' of America. Carrie, in one sense we are all common people in this country in that we have no inherited aristocracy. But, in a much more real sense we are a most uncommon people. Some of us go back in our family history to the very beginning of this nation and some of us are the first in our family's history to be Americans. In between is a mixture of those whose parents, grandparents, or great-grandparents migrated here from every corner of the world. But, we all have one thing in common, we or our ancestors had a quality that set us apart from others in those countries of our origin. That quality was a love of freedom and the courage to pull up roots and cross an ocean to start over again in a strange land, where in most cases even the language was foreign. Together we have created a nation and a people known as Americans—a very special breed by any measure.

"Yes, we have some problems and they aren't helped by penny-ante politicians who seek to advance themselves by casting blame on others for those problems. Some in the press and on radio and television have found it is easier to get attention by throwing rocks than by talking of our accomplishments. Don't let them sell America down the river—there is much to love and be proud of in our country.

"Oh, we've made mistakes—many of them, and some of them explain in part the very problems that upset you. For several decades we've drifted into a habit of turning to government for solutions when we should have worked out the answers ourselves. Young people think government should provide a free college education. Big corporations ask government to protect them and wind up complaining when government begins to make management decisions they should have made themselves. Labor asks congress to regulate wages and institute social reforms that labor and management should be working out between each other. Farmers and dairymen ask for help and end up with a program of government regimentation—told what they can plant and what prices they can charge. And, yes, your father, like everyone else, finds government taking half of his pay check to pay for all the bureaucracy it takes to do things we should be doing for ourselves.

"The meat shortage resulted in part from government interference that led to high feed and grain prices which in turn increased the cost of raising sheep, cattle, hogs, and poultry. Add to that, however, some acts of nature that can't be blamed on anyone. Two years ago, when the beef we are eating now were calves, there was a drought. These calves had to be fed hay and grain because the pasture had dried up. Thus, the farmers' cost in raising them doubled. Then last winter, we had severe storms in the West—one hundred million dollars worth of cattle were lost in one blizzard alone in Texas.

"On top of this (and this also explains the energy crisis) we are no longer the only people rich enough to eat meat, drive automobiles, and use oil and natural gas for heat and power. Japan, West Germany, and other nations are competing with us to buy things that are in short supply. Remember in the last fifteen years we increased our eating of beef from eighty-five pounds a year per person to one-hundred and sixteen pounds. Add to that the new markets in those other countries, and we just weren't producing enough beef. The same is true for oil and gas, as more people in the world could afford to drive cars.

"But, Carrie, we made it possible for those other people to live better—made it possible because Americans are the most generous people on earth.

"When World War I ended we cancelled much of the debt owed us by the European nations. We saved tens of millions from starving with outright gifts of every kind of supply. When World War II ended we literally rebuilt the industries and cities of not only our allies but of our enemies as well. Today the industrial power of West Germany and Japan bears a 'made in America' trademark. In the 1930s when Tokyo was leveled by an earthquake it was the United States that went in and helped keep them from starving. No matter where disaster has struck in the world—famine in

China and India, floods in Europe and Asia, etc., our country has gone to the rescue without asking anything in return.

"Can you find one instance of anyone coming to our aid? We, too, have had destructive floods on the Mississippi and the Ohio, tidal waves in the gulf, hurricanes and earthquakes. Never have we asked for help and none has been given.

"We speak of five major wars we've been in, but actually we've committed military forces to action 158 times in our 197-year history. Most of the time, we did so to help someone else—someone weaker whose freedom was threatened.

"Carrie, today young people are being taught a great many things that aren't true, and I'm afraid you are going to have to dig out the truth for yourself. Mistakes we've made—most of them well-intentioned ones—but we'll correct them, from the meat shortage to being in a position where we can be blackmailed by the Arab oil producers.

"Let's stop asking government to do things for us we should be doing for ourselves. Let's ask government to let us keep more of our own pay checks. And let us tell government and all those doom criers in our midst who want government to be a big brother to us all, that all we ask of freedom is freedom itself. This is still the one place on earth where a man can be whatever God intended he should be; where you can fly as high and as far as your own ability and effort will take you.

"You are absolutely right about this country and its dependence on men like your father. We read about knights in armor, or heroes doing battle, but the greatest unsung heroes in the world are men and women who get up in the morning, get you off to school, go to work, pay the bills, and voluntarily contribute to good causes in spite of high prices and higher taxes. They make this system work in spite of the demagogues and reformers who occasionally mess things up.

"And, Carrie, I have a hunch you'll be helping to keep that system working in a few more years. Your father should be a very proud man."

The same warm optimism came through in a letter to William R. Hammond of Schenectady, New York.

"Dear Bill:

"If I were 21, I believe, today, I would take a second and very good look at the world around me.

"If I had gained an impression in some classrooms, or from the daily fare doled out to us as news on too many TV newscasts, that we lived in a somewhat corrupt nation, that people were selfish and that all the old traditional values were long since outmoded, I would try to see if there wasn't another side to the coin. Optimism makes for a far better life than pessimism and there is much to be optimistic about in this land of ours.

"No matter how seamy the news may seem at times, this is a country of warm, generous people who seldom miss an opportunity to do good for their fellow man. In fact, the kindness of our people may have contributed to some of our troubles. We've tended to spoil our children and coddle our wrongdoers. But that's better than if the fault were the other way.

"I'd accept the help of those who wanted to help me and repay them by doing the same for others. I'd look with optimism and anticipation at a very exciting world that could be mine in the years ahead."

The environment and the ecology also drew letters from the younger generation. To Steven Hansch, editorial editor of *The Town Crier* in Santa Monica, he talked about "three kinds of pollution: actual, hysterical, and political:

"Hysterical pollution leads to political pollution with the result that all too often little or nothing gets done about actual pollution.

"Young people today can become a great force for good in overcoming the mistakes of the past and ensuring that their children will live in a cleaner world. The great need is for calm appraisal, recognition and evaluation of the real problem, and practical realism in solving it.

"Let me give you some examples of hysterical pollution. A letter arrives on my desk signed by an entire schoolroom of eight-year-olds. They beg me to save them from smothering to death before they can grow up. Obviously they had been frightened into mailing such a letter by some adult who should know better.

"Another letter, again from school children, expresses a belief that very soon all the redwood trees will have been cut down and replaced by plastic imitations.

"Now let's look at the facts about both of these examples.

"First, air pollution. Yes, we have problems in some areas, particularly our cities, but they are better than they were in the past. Martha Washington, when she was the first lady of our land, wrote a letter to her daughter about the terrible air pollution in Philadelphia. She said a majority of the city dwellers had eye infections from the smoke and gases in the air. Even Cicero in Ancient Rome wrote of the joy in getting out in the country away from the poisonous atmosphere of the city.

"Our problem today is caused largely by automobile exhaust. But not too long ago every home had a chimney belching coal smoke every hour of every winter day. We only discovered that autos were the cause of smog a few years ago, and now we are doing something about it. To-day's autos are only about a third as polluting as the cars of just eight or nine years ago, and our regulations require the manufacturers to virtually eliminate all pollutants by 1975.

"In the meantime we have political pollution. A politician wanting to attract attention introduces a bill to ban all autos if they aren't 100 percent clean within an impossibly short time. He knows that his proposed bill would force every car and truck off the road, close down the manufacturers, put every oil station out of business, and so on and on. Others have to rescue us from his demagoguery either by voting his bill down or by veto. He has made his splash, however, but in so doing has diverted the energies of those who are seriously trying to reduce air pollution.

"The same thing happens with regard to the trees. California over the years has done one of the outstanding jobs of preserving the great cathedral-like groves of redwoods. Almost 150,000 acres are now in our parks. Our lumber industry cutting the less spectacular commercial redwoods is rapidly approaching what is called 'sustained yield.' This means cutting no faster than the trees can grow back. But once again our energies are diverted from the real task of improving timber practices while we do battle with all sorts of unrealistic proposals. The plain truth is that we can have a lumber industry providing wood for home construction and furniture, and beautiful forests, too."

Molly C. Devine of Sacramento received this letter:

"I know you and your friends are impatient and want to get at the problem of pollution right away so my first answer won't make you too happy. Right now the main thing for all of you to do is study and learn about our environment but also about what we as people must have to make our lives enjoyable and fulfilling. This means jobs in which we earn our living, places to live, and power to heat our homes and light the lights.

"When you study, be sure to see all sides of each question and don't be frightened by those on either side of an argument who would have you believe the world will cave in if we don't do things their way. There isn't any problem we can't solve if we use common sense.

"Right now California is leading the nation in our efforts to solve the problems of pollution and environmental protection. This doesn't mean we can let up or that the problems will be solved overnight. We'll need your help in the years ahead when you are ready to take your place as citizens.

"But now in the meantime, why don't you look around you—I mean you and your friends, of course. See if you can find projects in your neighborhood or even farther afield. Several days ago the TV news showed a school class that picked a small creek here in Sacramento and spent the weekend clearing it of junk and tin cans to make it once again a sparkling, clear stream. There are sections of roadway and river banks littered with bottles and cans. Perhaps you can find someone who will lend a truck for hauling the debris away. Is there an empty lot that has become an eyesore—would the owner let you clean it up?

"I appreciate your wanting to help and know you can. I'd like to hear from you if you find a project."

In response to a letter from Tanya Tatum asking how he stood the pressures of office, he wrote:

"When I was first seeking this office, I made a campaign promise that I would make every decision based on the idea that I would never again run for public office. Now this didn't mean I wouldn't, but rather that in making decisions I would weigh them on what I honestly believed was right or wrong and not on how it might affect votes in some future election. I have kept that promise.

"The other thing, Tanya, when I first got here and sat at the desk where I'm sitting now, I found when almost every hour someone stood across the desk from me and said we have a problem, I had an almost irresistible desire to look over my shoulder at times as if there might be someone there I could pass the problem on to. I found out I was looking in the wrong direction. Obviously, the final decisions had to be made by me, but, Tanya, the help I have found is in turning to God and asking His help in prayer. I believe very much in the power of prayer and feel if you sincerely ask for His help, it is forthcoming. For me that has been the answer."

Not all of the governor's letters about youth were to them. Some went to parents. One parent wrote to him that "we have created a generation in which an alarming majority choose to wear the mask of indifference or intolerance. . . .

"It seems obvious that a frightening percentage of youth is running away from life.

"While talking to a youngster who was on dope, I asked what his parents thought of the way he chose to live. Consider, carefully, his reply: 'They don't give a damn what I do.' When asked why he thought that, he continued with, 'Not once has my old man or old lady said they would break my neck if they caught me smoking pot. They have never said they think my friends are creeps even though those thoughts are written all over their faces. I have NEVER heard my old man say, "Son, this is what I expect you to be like—this is how I expect you to act . . ." If they really cared, if they really loved me, they would help me. They don't give a damn and neither do I.'"

The governor's reply read:

"Let me get on the bandwagon with a counterpoint to the young pot smoker's plea or plaint. In New York recently at a dinner party a prominent editor sought the advice of several of us on 'What do you tell a teen-ager who uses pot?' I suspect he was really asking 'what do I do about my son?' I volunteered a few logical approaches, all of which he rejected. Finally (a little short of temper) I said, 'Why don't you tell him if you catch him with one of those things in his mouth you'll kick his bottom side up between his shoulders?' Of course, he rejected that too.

"Sandy, I'm convinced a lot of the college rioters are saying what your friend said. They really want someone to give them a set of rules and say 'don't step over that line.'"

A Sacramento school teacher wrote to him:

"I thought you might enjoy a little humor today which happened in my kindergarten class.

"I was briefing my class on the field trip we were to take the following day. One of the places scheduled to visit was the governor's mansion.

"'Does anyone know who is the governor of California?' I asked.

"(Complete silence)

"'Oh, come now children, you know his name. Ronald——?' (I hinted)

"Instantly twenty-three hands shot up and twenty-three voices shouted triumphantly—

"'RONALD MCDONALD!'"

The governor thanked her, saying "I did get a kick out of it. I guess television just has more power than any of us know.

"I'll return the favor by telling you of the teacher who taught her class about magnets and their properties and then several weeks later gave a test and asked them what it was that was spelled with six letters, began with an M and picked up things. Eighty-seven percent of the class said 'mother.' The true television anecdote, however, is the child who told her mother she liked her better than the other leading brands.

"Thanks, again, and please give my greetings to your class. Tell them I don't mind being Ronald McDonald at all."

The governor also presumed upon his friendship with the president on behalf of young constituents.

"Dear Mr. President:

"I am enclosing a letter regarding a special tour you provided for some of our mutual constituents. The son, Bob, he refers to had his eighteenth birthday. He is a paraplegic, paralyzed from the chest down in an accident about four years ago, a high school senior. The Gibsons are strong, loyal Republicans.

"Now, having said thanks, I reward you with another chore if you see fit to do it. A little nine-year-old girl, Carol Ann Poitevin, Painted Valley Stables, 2940 Chestnut Avenue, Long Beach, California, 90806, has a mare stabled at the horse farm next door to the Western White House. It is due to foal momentarily. Carol feels this makes her a next-door neighbor to you. She is sure you must have reached over the fence and petted her mare sometime when you were out there. She would like a note from her neighbor that she could keep."

Here is one other letter to a parent who was also a friend.

"Dear Bing:

"Last Friday, as you've no doubt seen in the news, I had a rather busy time at the University of California at Santa Cruz. There is no need for me to go into the sad experience of seeing students on that beautiful campus rioting, threatening physical harm to the regents assembled there, and cursing the regents with profanity and unrepeatable obscenities. Enough to say—it happened.

"But out of all this came one bright moment, at least for me. On the bus tour of the campus, students have been assigned to the buses as guides. I found myself seated beside one of the nicest, most ladylike young women one could hope to meet—your daughter. After hearing her good common-sense reaction to all that was going on, I finally had to ask how she had been able to maintain such a sense of values in the atmosphere so prevalent there. She stated very simply, 'That's the way my mother and father raised me.'

"You must be very proud and you have every right to be."

An eleven-year-old girl who wanted a horse desperately

wrote to the governor explaining that her father could not afford to keep it at the stables "and I cannot keep it in my yard in Long Beach." At her father's suggestion she asked "if I could graze my horse on your pasture in Malibu. My dad said it might be tax deductible. I am eleven years old and my dad said you would understand. Please Mr. Reagan write back soon so I will know the answer."

The governor wrote back:

"I certainly can understand how you feel; horses have been a large part of my life and I love them as you do. But your father has brought up a very important point. They can't be stored away in a garage like a bike until you feel like going for a ride, and there is an ongoing expense day in and day out. Unfortunately we have had to sell our ranch so I can't be of help in the way you suggested.

"But let me make some other suggestions. First of all, not owning a horse needn't keep you from riding and learning about horses. As a matter of fact, in the cavalry (which is where I learned to ride) you weren't assigned a horse of your own until you had learned to ride on many different horses—a different one every day.

"You have many years ahead of you to enjoy riding and to have your own horse. Indeed you'll know too the sorrow of saying goodbye because we do outlive our horses. Now and for the next few years, why don't you go to a stable (you probably ride at one now), ride many horses, learn to know their differences, and learn all you can about their care? Then when you are a few years older you might discover you can have a horse of your own, and you'll know better the exact kind of horse you want.

"At that time you can very probably make an arrangement with someone or some stable so that you can board or pasture your horse in return for helping with theirs. You'll know enough about the care of horses that you'll have something to offer.

"Being a father myself, I know how very much your father would like to be able to help you realize your dream, but sometimes we have to wait for the good things. If it will help to know this, I didn't have a horse of my own until after I was grown up. You'll do better than that, so keep on riding and studying."

A young man suggested that a way to create rapport with the younger generation would be for the governor to start riding a motorcycle. The governor declined. "I . . . think I'll have to stick to horseback riding. You see, there is the matter of security. When I go any place, I'm one of a group. We might look like Hell's Angels with all of us out there on motorcycles."

A campaign held by a high-school girl to save four acres of land for an ecological park brought this note from Governor Reagan. "I wish more people who are talking about saving the environment had your great good common sense." Enclosed was a check for $50.

Sometimes letters were never sent. A young California constituent wrote asking for a picture and a phone call. The governor dictated the letter, then did not sign it. Instead across the bottom he wrote to me: "Just send the picture. I'll call him—I'm a sucker."

And that is true—but only if having a soft heart makes a person "a sucker."

Laurie Rothe and Jeffrey Trauberman, the editors of *Embers,* a publication of Wayne Valley Senior High in Wayne, New Jersey, wrote to Governor Reagan asking him to write an article advising the school's graduating seniors. "You've taken quite a chance," he warned them, "risking a detailed and nostalgic accounting of things as they used to be, or a denunciation of things as they are."

But then he sent the following letter to the graduating seniors:

"Your editors have asked me to attempt some advice, particularly for those of you who are now leaving high school. Since all of us enjoy giving advice, I accepted their invitation with delight; also, I might add, with a feeling of appreciation for what I consider a very great honor.

"Now, after many false starts, and a waste basket full of wadded up rejects, I have discovered this is more of a challenge than an opportunity. Advising an individual with whom you are acquainted is one thing; generalizing across the generation gap is quite another.

"All of the clichés about entering a new phase in your lives have been strengthened by the change in voting laws. You are about to come into your inheritance of citizenship as full participants in the social structure—call it establishment if you will—virtually coincident with receiving your diplomas. I'm not sure that you greet this prospect with joyous anticipation.

"A consortium of doom-cryers made up of journalists, commentators, writers, and yes, a goodly portion of the educational and intellectual community, have conspired together to paint a picture of a sick society in a polluted land where money-grubbing materialism has replaced spiritual values. Admittedly, the world you inherit is less than perfect. Not all the problems of human misery have been solved. Poverty and inequality of opportunity still exist; prejudice and bigotry have not been erased from every heart; and war, man's greatest stupidity, still takes place.

"But let my first advice to you be, look beyond the picket signs and leaflets; check the doom-cryers' pronouncements against the facts. Each generation stands on the shoulders of the one that has gone before, and as a result, each succeeding generation can see farther and more clearly because of the height from which they gaze. If you will look from unprejudiced eyes, you will discover ours is not a sick society, and there is much to be proud of in this land and much to love.

"Man has known only a few moments of freedom in his entire history, and most of those moments have been ours. Half the economic activity in all history has taken place in America, and we have shared our wealth more widely than any people who ever lived. Ninety percent of the people in our land lived in poverty at the time of my birth; today it is ten percent. More than two-thirds of our people lived in substandard housing; today, it is less than ten percent. Our poor have miracles of convenience not even a king could afford a hundred years ago. Ninety-nine percent of our homes have refrigerators and gas or electric stoves; ninety-five percent have television; more than ninety percent have telephones. In my lifetime we have eliminated diseases which had plagued man for thousands of years. I've already lived ten years longer than my life expectancy when I was born.

"Yes, we have ethnic and racial problems, but we've made progress. We have done more in a single lifetime to advance the dignity of man than had been done in all the long climb from the swamp to the stars. When my generation left high school we took our place in a society that didn't even know it had a racial problem. I'm proud that we were the ones who said, 'This isn't good enough.' There is still a lot to be done, but also we've done a lot. In America today a higher percentage of our minority young men and women go to college than the percentage of white youth in any other country in the world.

"We are in an ugly war, but not because we don't love peace, and certainly not because we have an aggressive, hostile nature. My generation has known war four times and has learned to hate it. We long for peace, but know that longing is not enough. In this disturbed world it is possible to love peace, to strive for peace, and find yourselves in war. If this is hard for you to accept, ask yourselves what kind of a world you'd be living in if another generation had not been willing to bleed its finest young men into the sands of Omaha Beach, the mud of Normandy, and a thousand coral atolls up and down the Pacific. The inescapable truth is that the lasting values, the things which go to make up what we call civilization, have always been those things for which men have been willing to die if need be.

"With your idealism, your youth and energy, you are going to make this a better world. In your lifetime you will most likely see cancer eliminated, poverty further reduced, and those last pockets of bigotry and prejudice wiped out. You may in your lifetime realize man's dream of a world without war. Please keep striving for that, but not under the delusion that peace is worth any price.

"Challenge the mores and customs of the past, but do not discard them simply because they are of the past. A cynical few would have you turn from old truths and moral standards accumulated by man through the ages. Select carefully the things you would discard. No nation which has outgrown its God has ever lived to write additional pages of history. This nation is in need of a spiritual reawakening, and a reaffirmation of trust in God. This can begin with a return to simple morality—a revival of honor and integrity in our everyday lives.

"If I read your generation correctly, you've been turned off by hypocrisy and dirty politics; you yearn for leaders who will be above partisanship and personal gain. Well, your leaders are among you now—presidents, governors, senators and congressmen, supreme court justices—how will you know which ones they are when the time comes to choose? Do you think they can cheat now, shave the rules, choose the laws they'll obey or disregard, and then by some magic become men and women who will make decisions on the basis of what is morally right or wrong?

"One generation can change the course of history; can once again ensure that this nation will be a shining golden hope for all mankind. An older generation hopes with all its heart you'll do this."

Love Letters, More or Less

While this is supposed to be a book of letters by and from Ronald Reagan there is a group of letters *to* him that I think must be included. These are letters from children, mostly written in his early years as governor. They are all written very seriously, but some make me want to laugh, and others make my eyes misty.

For a long time the governor wanted to find a way to share them with other Americans. Perhaps through this little book people, who otherwise would never have the opportunity to see them, will have a chance to share the pleasure that was the governor's when he received them.

"Dear Governor:
"I remember when you were an actor. Now I see you have changed.
"I liked you better as an actor.
"Your ex-fan,
"John"

"Dear Mr. Reagan:
"My daddy says that since you became governor, many things have changed.
"Two ice cream men used to come down our street every day—but not any more. One of the trucks was pulled by
175

a horse. Did you take him to a race track or just change the streets they go down?

"Cindy"

"Dear Governor Reagan:

"Could you come and have a barbecue with us at our house. Our pool is 75 feet by 40 feet.

"You may, also, bring your family but my Mom says you can't spend the night."

"Dear Governor Reagan:

"Yesterday I saw a bumper sticker that said 'Ronald Reagan eats peanut butter.'

"I want to know if it's true.

"Kathy Johnson

"P.S. No offense"

"Dear Sir:

"February is Citizenship Month.

"What ideals, habits, and attitudes did you develop as a third grader which helped make you the outstanding citizen you are today?

"Thank you.

"Love,

"Becky"

"Thank you very much for just the information I needed. But there is one thing I don't understand. Specifically, what are you doing about it? Thanks again.

"I am very grateful for your answering my request. The signature on the letter you sent back, your own, I will keep it until I die, and I really mean it.

"From Margie"

"Dear Governor:

"How come when politicians have meetings about pollution and conservation, they are always in smoke-filled rooms?"

"Dear Sir:

"It is wonderful to know you are governor of California. This proves that any citizen can run and be elected."

"Dear Mr. Reagan:

"You are doing a terrific and outstanding job—and I am proud you were elected governor of Ohio.

"Your friend,

"Jackie"

"To my Governor:

"My name is Andy Peterson. I'm in the 8th grade and 13 years old. On my way to school I walk on 28th Street. When I get to the corner to go across, I can't see if any cars are coming because the trees are so big and lots of cars are parked on the side. This is very dangerous and before I get killed, I think something should be done about it.

"Thank you.

"Leslie Jamison" [sic]

"Dear Governor Reagan:

"I'm sorry you were killed last night on TV.

"My brother said you were faking. Is that true?

"Love,

"Lisa"

"Dear Governor:

"Some of us would like to know if a teacher can hit a child on the hands with a ruler.

"I say the teacher doesn't have the right to.

"Maria

"P.S. If my writing is bad—it's because my hand is sore."

"Dear Governor:

"I am a new citizen. My whole family is, too. We come from Mexico.

"More than anything I want a great American flag. I will love and care for it.

"Your new friend who loves you,
"Maria
"P.S. I will also treat it with respect."

"Dear Honorable Sir:
"I want to know if you think diagramming sentences is important later on in life. In fact our whole class wants to know if you had to diagram sentences in the seventh grade.
"Did it help you to speak?
"Sincerely,
"Wally
"P.S. I hate diagramming sentences."

"Dear Sir:
"I am in the 4th grade. This is a test on how to write letters. I think it's nobody's business how people write letters.
"Will you kindly do something about this?
"I am—
"Paul Turner"

"Dear Mr. Governor:
"Have you ever heard of the Dumbarton Bridge? If you have, could you maybe change the name, please? It would sure help me with the kids at school.
"Yours truly,
"Betsy Barton
"P.S. If you can't change the name—could you just take off the *Dum*?"

"Dear Mr. Reagan:
"I would like a picture of you and your family. I see you and your family on TV and in the newspapers and magazines. I know all about you. I am a big fan of yours. Thanks.
"Yours truly,
"Pam
"P.S. On the back name the people in the picture."

"Dear Governor Reagan:

"I need information right now on your running for president.

"Are you going to do it? What are your chances? Will you run?

"Thank you.

"Danny

"P.S. If you don't know can you give me an address where I could find out?"

"Dear Governor:

"What are you going to do to help California's Indians?

"Love

"Billy

"P.S. My father is an Orthodontist."

"Mr. Reagan:

"Before I get started—I warn you, I'm only a girl of ten—and a Democrat, too!

"Yours

"Lori"

"Dear Governor Reagan:

"I wrote you once before about having to go to school on my birthday—and nothing happened.

"My next birthday is a month away and I am wondering what your plans are.

"Let me hear from you soon.

"Jeff"

"To Mr. Ronald Reagan

"I pray for you every day because Mom thinks you need it.

"From Margie King"

A National Spokesman Emerges

RONALD REAGAN SERVED two four-year terms as governor of California, taking office in January 1967, and leaving in January 1975. Believing two terms as governor of the largest state were enough, he refused entreaties by friends and political allies to run for a third term. This was in keeping with a campaign promise he made as a candidate in 1966 that he would limit himself to two terms.

Governor Reagan subsequently rejected efforts to have him run for governor again in 1978, although most political experts believed he was the only California Republican who could have beaten his Democratic successor, Edmund G. Brown, Jr.

After leaving office Ronald Reagan became a radio commentator, speaking on a wide range of matters of interest to the public on 300 radio stations around the nation.

In addition he quickly became one of the most sought-after public speakers, not only for political affairs but also for business conventions and similar gatherings.

These activities were shelved during 1976, but he resumed them after the 1976 presidential campaign and also began writing a twice-a-week newspaper column syndicated in more than one hundred newspapers.

Radio and his newspaper column account in large part for his continuing heavy load of mail. In responding personally to much of it Governor Reagan has gone on record on many different issues.

Following are excerpts of letters that tell his positions on issues of general interest:

Prayer in school: "I have always thought that a voluntary period of silent prayer in schools could hardly violate our constitutional protection regarding separation of church and state. My fear is that, with the total ignoring of religion, morality, and ethics in the schools, our children are likely to grow up believing that morality and ethical behavior have no place in everyday life when, in fact, our nation was founded by those who came here in search of freedom to worship. It just seems to me that Mrs. (Madelyn) O'Hare has done more than protest against having religion forced upon her son. She has, in turn, forced her view upon the rest of us."

Letter to Mrs. Jack Wallace
of Tulsa, Oklahoma, 1977

Victimless crime: "In my experience, I've found that some who appear to be victimless do, indeed, impose on others, even if indirectly. Another facet of this has to do with my belief that man-made law should not supersede a higher natural law. We should not make legal that which is patently immoral."

Volunteer Army: "On the Volunteer Army, I'm totally opposed to a peace-time draft, but believe that the draft is essential in time of war."

Letter to William R. Rausch
of Seattle, Washington, 1975

ERA: "It is true I'm not in support of the ERA, but not for the reasons given by TIME. I'm totally in favor of correcting any and all inequities—by statute. However, based on legal advice I sought and received while governor, I believe a 'simple' amendment to the Constitution could be used to eliminate many legitimate advantages women now enjoy; advantages having to do with home and child support as well as work rules based on physiological differences between the sexes."

Abortion: "As for abortion, my position is simply that interrupting a pregnancy *does* take a human life. This should only be allowed in the context of our Judeo-Christian tradition that allows the taking of a life only in defense of our own. Thus a mother-to-be has the right to kill her own unborn child only to protect her own life and health.

It seems ironic that today's laws recognize the right of the unborn child to own property but not the right to protect its own life."

Letter to Ethel M. Wood
of Cleveland, Ohio, 1975

National security and the press: "I want the people informed, as you do. I don't want there to be shelters behind which bureaucracy or elected representatives can hide under the guise of security, but I also don't want the communications media to irresponsibly expose matters that do inform the potential enemy and thus help him in what I think is a plan and the determination to dominate the world."

Letter to Martin Radoff,
of Encino, California, 1975

The CIA and individual freedom: "I doubt that we have any real disagreement about the errors made by CIA agents and individuals when they went beyond duty and violated civil rights and common morality.

"Perhaps we differ on what I see as a certain secrecy that I believe is imperative if any intelligence force is to accomplish its mission.

"I still feel strange taking this side of the argument because, frankly, I feel government has gone far beyond its rights in literally dozens of areas. Indeed, I think individual freedom is endangered more by agencies such as the Internal Revenue Service, the EPA, the various consumer agencies, OSHA, and countless other bureaus practicing what Cicero called 'the arrogance of officialdom.' We are a nation of laws, but we are presumed innocent if charged with breaking one of those laws. Not so with bureaucratic regulations. If we break a regulation, we are guilty as charged, and the bureau or agency bringing the charge is judge, jury, and executioner. Isn't this a situation which should cause us concern?"

Letter to Martin Radoff
of Encino, California, 1975

Business: "We have turned to government more and more (for answers that could better be provided in the market place) until we have shackled business and industry with so many restrictions, nit-picking, and regulations, punitive taxes that we can no longer compete in the world market. Thus, we can't expand industry to provide the jobs our people need.

"Remember, business doesn't pay taxes. It collects them for government. But it must pass those taxes on as part of the cost of production. So, they end up in the price of the product with the customer paying them. When we make business collect too much, we price business out of the market. None of the other leading industrial nations do as much of this to their industries as we do."

Wage and price controls: "Why don't we impose wage and price controls? Because they don't work and never have. Hammurabi tried them in Babylon 5000 years ago and they failed. Emperor Diocletian imposed them on Rome and almost bankrupted the empire. They distract the natural markets supplying the people's needs to bootleg prices. England had them in effect following the Napoleonic wars and if it hadn't been for smugglers, the people would have starved. The controls here in 1971 are part of what caused our troubles today."

Letter to Capt. Wayne P. Spiegel
Air Force, 1975

Unemployment: "With regard to unemployment, I believe government should offer incentives to business designed to encourage creation of jobs, instead of spending the money to create temporary public jobs which usually wind up in an unnecessary expansion of the local public payroll on a permanent basis. The labor department has no inventory of where job skills are surplus or areas where those job skills are in short supply. In job training the government has been a colossal failure. The best method is 'on the job' training. What if the same funds were used to encourage business to take on and train the unskilled?"

Letter to Ralph Krueger
of Richard, Virginia, 1975

The American government: "I believe in this system and don't believe it has ever failed us. We have failed it many times. When a national poll reveals that only 46 percent of the people can name their U.S. congressman and that, of those who know the name 86 percent can't tell you anything more about him (how he votes, what he believes, etc.), we are not practicing government by the people. And we are failing the system.

"I began my citizenship as a New Deal Democrat and only switched parties when, in my opinion, the leadership of my party departed from the Democratic traditions of states' rights, free trade, and individual freedom."

Letter to Janice Harrison
Fayetteville, Tennessee, 1977

Federal spending: ". . . except in times of emergency such as war, the federal government must have a balanced budget."

Constitutional amendment, suggested
in letter to Herb Wells,
Whittier, California, 1976

This and that: "Yes, I favor women in politics. However, I do think that all appointments should be based on someone's qualifications rather than sex. I am in favor of capital punishment but against legalized gambling. Congress should, I feel, favorably consider Puerto Rico for statehood, if the People of Puerto Rico initiate such action."

Letter to John Doak
Tulsa, Oklahoma, 1977

Vietnam: "While I was not necessarily in favor of sending ground troops to Vietnam, I felt very strongly that once we committed our boys to fight overseas, we should have put our entire resources behind them and let them win the war. I've always said that the only war worth fighting for is one that's also worth winning. Whether we were right or wrong in our commitment to Vietnam, the truth is that we did not live up to it."

Letter to Mrs. J. E. Sorrells
Ira, Texas, 1975

The draft: "I have always favored the idea of a volunteer army. I have never believed in peacetime conscription."

Letter to Tony Castle
Los Angeles, California, 1977

The Black vote: ". . . the Republican Party must work to show Black Americans that our party has something to offer them. On behalf of the Republican candidate in the last election, however, may I point out that the limited amount permitted candidates for campaign spending dictates strategy to a great extent. Knowing that the Black community normally votes Democratic, it's hard to justify spending the limited funds available on what is an outside chance of winning votes.

"This, of course, doesn't mean you don't want those votes or that you should give up trying. I've always believed that the time to take our campaign on such a mission is in the off year, when there is no election at stake."

Letter to Dwight F. Holloway
Suitland, Maryland, 1977

One-term presidency: "I have long felt this country needs more than anything a one-term president who will take on the problems with no thought of the next election."

Letter to R. G. Friedman
Fort Lauderdale, Florida, 1975

The Middle East: "I have long felt that the villain in the piece is the Soviet Union—stirring up trouble as it has in so many other corners of the world. My own view has been that the United States, by displacing the Soviet influence, could bring a settlement in the Middle East by recognizing how much right there is on both sides.

"Perhaps it is oversimplification on my part, but it seems to me that the difficulty with restoring the captured territory hinges on the reluctance of the Arab states to acknowledge the existence of Israel."

Letter to William A. Walmsley
San Jose, California, 1977

Communists: "There is no doubt that their policy is to move in wherever there is an opening. Whenever there is a division—racial problems, labor movements, etc.—they do their best to keep the pot boiling . . .

". . . Right now there is *no* congressional committee left to investigate subversion. All have been eliminated. We need a public demand for the reinstatement of a committee such as the onetime 'House Committee to Investigate Un-American Activities.'

". . . a direct assault on domestic communism today would be premature. We need the factual evidence a congressional investigation could provide."

Letter to Paul E. Richards
San Diego, California, 1977

Soul-Searching Leads to Decision

RONALD REAGAN ANNOUNCED on November 20, 1975, that he was a candidate for the 1976 Republican presidential nomination. He read the following statement at a 10 A.M. press conference held in the ballroom of the National Press Club in Washington, D.C.:

"There are moments in a nation's history when the people become aware that only a sharp change of course will solve the problems besetting them. We are in such a moment. Ironically it was in another troubled time more than four decades ago that we set in motion some of the forces which have brought us to this present time of decision.

"In the depression years there were those who promised to overcome hard times. Franklin Delano Roosevelt embarked on a course that made bold use of government to ease the pain. Although some of these measures seemed to work he was soon moved to utter a warning—'we have built up new instruments of *public* power in the hands of the people's government . . . but in the hands of political puppets of an economic autocracy such power would provide shackles for the liberties of our people.'

"Unfortunately his warning went unheeded. Today there is an economic autocracy because of government's interference in and control of the economy. The *traditional*

187

relationship between the people and their government has been greatly changed.

"Over these past four decades political puppets of this autocracy have persuaded first one group, then another to turn to government for answers to problems it was never designed to solve. Social Security tinkering led to costly failures which were then overlaid by even costlier failures until we have a government of such complexity it grows in size beyond the consent of the governed. It confiscates 44 cents out of every dollar earned by those who work and produce, but even this isn't enough. The rest of us must live within a budget based on our income even though our dollars buy less each day than they did the day before. Government recognizes no such restraint. It causes an ever-worsening inflation by piling up repeated deficits which destroy the value of our savings and pensions, making it impossible for many to own homes and more difficult to provide goods and clothing for the family. Indeed government is the costliest item in the family budget, greater than food, shelter, and clothing combined. Its great appetite for money chokes off the supply for the free sector of our economy, reducing it's ability to grow and create jobs. And for all of this we get intrusion into our lives and a network of regulations which interfere with our ability to make decisions on our own. In the area that is truly government's responsibility, our protection, we find we are no longer safe in our homes or on the streets of our own neighborhoods.

"This didn't happen all at once. Idealists became autocrats as they attempted to legislate and regulate us into a state of human perfection. They sought the impossible and of course failed, but there has been no learning from their mistakes so they go on repeating them. Today these well-intentioned autocrats—elitists of Big Government and yes, Big Labor and Big Business are insulated from the people who really keep America moving.

"Alexander Solzhenitsyn tells us that when a new prisoner is thrown into a cell with Soviet political prisoners the common greeting is, 'Are you from freedom?'

"Well our prison is economic but born of politics, and

it has sapped us of spirit, replacing our confidence and pride with false guilt as it erodes our liberty.

"We aren't helped by the words of foreign demogogues who would rather find in us a scapegoat than face up to the task of building their new nations as we once built ours.

"Standing here in this place it gives me no pleasure to say our own capital city symbolizes our economic prison. It has proven it is not the solver of our problems. It *is* the problem. The American dream has somewhere been mislaid. We have to hope and believe the loss is temporary. Millions of Americans across this land still live by that dream and are determined to keep and expand their freedom and their independence. They know that to do this they must reduce the power centralized in Washington.

"Over these past ten months going to almost every part of this country I've seen this in the faces of our citizens and heard it in their voices. We hunger for a sense of mission; to have once again a pride in our capacity to perform great deeds.

"Our children have heard too many political and economic myths in too many classrooms and all of us have heard too much of political demagoguery. The people are the best agents of their own destinies. Armed with the truth they will meet any challenge and make any sacrifice.

"They do not lack in courage or heroism. We had proof of this a short time ago when we saw on our TV screens, young Americans, the product of this way of ours, return from years of savage captivity, unbroken, heads held high, asking God's blessing on us as they saluted the flag.

"The hour is late for turning our nation toward a new, constructive course. To make government again our servant and to bring back to a human, understandable scale control by us of our own destiny. I am convinced that the great strength of the American people still glows and can be reignited to be the beacon of freedom it once was. Because I believe this so strongly I have come here to say that I shall be a candidate for the Republican nomination for the presidency of the United States. These are not easy words for me to say nor has the decision to say them been easy. I have some idea of the enormous task ahead and know I will need the help of all those who have urged me to do this.

"In the weeks and months ahead I'll be discussing in detail my ideas and my belief that Americans can once again try the untried with confidence in our energy, our ingenuity, and yes in our spiritual heritage.

"Later today I'll visit some of the states whose primaries I shall enter. There will of course be others as well.

"I make one promise and one only to the people of America—Republicans, Democrats, and Independents—and I make it also to myself. The principles I believe in and which I'll be discussing in these coming months will not be changed or compromised to meet so-called political realities."

But the decision to run did not come easily to Governor Reagan. He had several reservations.

First of all he did not relish the idea of running against a sitting Republican president, even an appointed one, because he has always viewed himself as a party unifier, not a party divider.

Secondly, he did not wish to run if President Ford were going to do the kind of job he, Ronald Reagan, thought should be done.

He put these thoughts in a July 14, 1975, letter to Joseph Coors, a longtime friend and supporter. "But here is the real argument against an early announcement; look at what has happened to the president's approval rating in recent weeks. If he is going to turn (really turn) and do what we all want, where would I be as an announced candidate if conservatives suddenly discovered they were satisfied with the present incumbent?" He added that "we must continue to press forward until we discover if the new conservatism is either for real or is campaign tactics. If the former, we will have achieved something; if the latter, we must be in a position to move."

He concluded, "Joe, I know there is a decision to be made, but I honestly don't know what that decision will be. I'm not being indecisive or reluctant. I just don't have the information I need to make that decision which is, mainly, how deep is that grass-roots wave of rebellion. The plan is to find out and, if it is there, then to go the primary route. There is a game plan, and I feel I must stay with it."

The governor wrote that letter just a few days after Senator Paul Laxalt had announced the formation of a "Citizens for Reagan" exploratory committee, the purpose of which was to see if there was significant national support for a Reagan run for the presidency.

Another thing had always bothered the governor, too. He had a genuine belief that, as he put it, "the office should seek the man." In other words, a man shouldn't run for president just as an ego trip; there should be a legitimate and significant demand for his leadership from the people. The purpose of the exploratory committee was to find out if there was such a demand.

And there was still another reason, which he explained succinctly in a letter to Ralph Tipton of Lisle, Illinois, on August 25, 1975. "Tip, I just can't make the early decision you suggest. For one reason, I have to be sure, or reasonably so, that I offer the best opportunity for victory. The principal consideration has to be that the Democrats do not occupy the White House. I think you'll agree that we don't have the information we need to that answer just yet."

He put it a little differently on September 24 of that year in a letter to W. P. Spofford of Pensacola, Fla. "That decision (to run), I might add, will be made on the basis of what is best for this country as nearly as I'm able to make such an evaluation."

There were those who, before his announcement, wanted him to explore the "third party" route. Douglas W. Woods of Abingdon, Illinois, urged him not to rule out the possibility of a third party. On October 29, 1975, Governor Reagan responded: "As for forming a third party, I can understand how you, and for that matter a great many others, feel about a third party possibly offering an answer to the problems confronting the nation. At the same time, however, may I point out an unhappy fact of history: that in the main, third parties have failed in their purpose. Indeed, all too often they only succeed in dividing the vote of those with one philosophy and contribute to the election of those whose philosophy they oppose.

"Before we give up on a two-party system that has served us well over much of our history, I favor an all-out try to create what might be called a new second party. With the Democratic party in the hands of a leadership totally out of step with its own rank-and-file membership, shouldn't we try to present a Republican party which truly represents the thinking of the great majority of Americans, Republicans, Democrats, and Independents?

"There is no reason why the Republican party should not return to its basic philosophy. Let it make plain to all the people it stands for fiscal responsibility, limited government, and a common-sense approach to national security, as well as to safety in our own neighborhoods. And, let it declare most emphatically there will be no compromising of principle for political expediency.

"I believe it's worth a try."

About the same time the governor wrote a letter to his friend, Senator Jesse Helms (R-N.C.) that, while it did not talk about the presidency, indicated his concern for the nation. It was written just before the opening of the 1975 North Carolina State Republican convention.

"I wish I could be there to hear your message to the Republican Convention. This truly is a time 'for all good men and women to come to the aid of the party.' What is more important is that our party come to the aid of the country.

"It is peculiarly appropriate that the Democrats will hold their National Convention in New York City. Let them see at first hand what the full implementation of their philosophy can accomplish. For the rest of us, let New York be a warning of what will befall the nation if we lack the courage and determination to turn from our present path.

"A great bloc of Americans today disenchanted with politics as usual look for leadership and the means to restore common sense to government. Our party can offer the vehicle, the machinery by which their hopes and dreams can be realized.

"You and a little band of your colleagues have been holding the ramparts for quite a while now. It's about time you were sent reinforcement. Heaven only knows the irresponsible majority you've been opposing has neither the will or the skill to do what has to be done."

Ronald Reagan has always accepted the support of a wide range of Americans in the belief that if they support him they are accepting his philosophy of government and not the other way around. On October 6, 1975, in a letter to Hugh Gregg, former governor of New Hampshire, who had just agreed to accept the chairmanship of Citizens for Reagan in New Hampshire, Governor Reagan explained this. The letter also tells of his feelings about New Hampshire and its significance as the state with the first primary.

"As I approach the time to announce my final decision, I can't tell you how pleased I am that you have accepted the chairmanship of 'Citizens for Reagan' in New Hampshire. As I told you when we met last month, I feel strongly that any serious candidate for president must run and do well in the New Hampshire primary if he is to be regarded as a bona fide contender for his party's nomination.

"I am grateful to Governor Thomson, a good personal friend, for the support he has offered to me. However, he knows and agrees that I should not be looking to him to put your campaign organization together and to make it function. He agrees that you and your committee must be able independently to develop an organization on my behalf which will assure a victory. And, of course, we all agree that I must be able to demonstrate the ability to stand on my own two feet in New Hampshire if an effective nation-wide effort is to be mounted.

"Finally, and I'm sure you will agree with this, any campaign for the presidency must reflect my philosophy, my views, and my proposals for leading our nation. Those who choose to support me will do so because they have accepted my positions and not the other way around.

"At this moment, I am convinced that my candidacy not only would not be divisive, but would be welcomed as a means of stirring up interest and reinvigorating our party.

"I'm looking forward to seeing you shortly and hope that we will be working closely together during the next several months in support of those things in which we both believe."

One reason that made Ronald Reagan hesitate about running for his party's presidential nomination was the fear that he would be considered divisive by many Republicans.

During his entire political career he had striven to be a party unifier. For that reason he had laid down a rule for himself not to take sides in primary elections. It was a rule that he seldom violated, because he felt that after a primary struggle for any office somebody had to be there to bring together the warring factions. That was a role he adopted early in his political career and always felt comfortable with.

Now, suddenly here he was thinking about attempting to wrest his party's presidential nomination away from a sitting president. True, President Ford had never been elected to that position, but he was president and many Republicans who might have otherwise preferred Governor Reagan were supporting Ford for that reason alone.

But Reagan made peace with himself on this particular issue well before he finally decided to run. In a letter to Mrs. Donal Irion of New Hartford, New York, he explained his stand.

"Let me assure you that if I should decide to seek the nomination, I will abide by the party's eleventh commandment, 'Thou shalt not speak ill of any other Republican,' and confine my campaign to issues and philosophy. I do not see how providing Republicans with a choice could cause disunity among the ranks. To the contrary, I think it would stimulate interest and actively involve Republicans who may feel disgruntled and alienated with the prospect of closed convention. Don't forget we are faced with an unprecedented situation in that both our president and vice president were not chosen by the party.

"While we may differ on how to achieve it, my objective is the same as yours—a strong Republican party. I am convinced that the apathy we find among voters today is not so much due to a disillusioned constituency but rather the dissimilation of the two parties. In the hope to 'broaden' our base and to find greater voter appeal, the Republican philosophy has been watered down beyond recognition. I think it is time we return to our conservative principles and raise a banner, giving everyone who shares our belief a cause to work and fight for."

On November 20, 1975, he raised that banner and thus began a national crusade that, despite a setback in August of 1976, continues to this day.

Looking Back

AFTER GOVERNOR REAGAN lost the Republican nomination to Gerald Ford, he received, not unexpectedly, a flood of political correspondence. Writers, both friends and strangers, offer their views and advice, and take him to task for things he allegedly had done or said, or not done or not said.

William Loeb, publisher of the Manchester, New Hampshire, *Union Leader*, wrote him immediately following the 1976 election: "You would have had many more votes if you had another label besides Republican." Loeb envisioned a new party of "producers." He said, "I am talking about the fellows at the bench and at the drafting table, the doctors and the architects—all the hard-working people who make the things go around in this country."

The governor responded: "We may not be too far apart in our thinking on the party situation. Maybe I'm calling what you'd call a new third party a new second party. I'd like one last go at making our platform the basis for a party statement of principles. Then, with that as a rallying point I'd like to see if we could take that solid conservative majority of grassroots Republicans and set out to gather in, on a kind of merger basis, those independents and disaffected Democrats who subscribe to those principles . . . and, if it will be helpful and give more of a merger feeling, h--l yes, change the party's name."

He added, ". . . at the grassroots level the solid corps of conservatism is already to be found in our party. If it doesn't work, the other road is still open. One thing for sure—no more appeasing of the Ripon wing. They don't belong and they've never done us any good."

To Walter Lloyd of Fresno, California, he wrote: "I believe we must have a rebuilt or revitalized Republican party, not a third party. . . . the biggest single gathering of conservatives is to be found in the Republican party and . . . we should build on that, not scrap it and face starting over."

Governor Reagan is not one of those who believes the Republican party should broaden its base by liberalizing its principles. In a letter to W. B. Allen of Claremont, California, Governor Reagan wrote: "I assure you, I'm not one of those who advocates broadening the base of our party by outpromising the Democrats and keeping our people black and white and separated into voting blocs."

He wrote to Joe Kimmel, Jr., of Davenport, Iowa, that "we are in complete agreement. The party must expand, but only by seeking support of those who subscribe to our philosophy."

However, he told Col. John Regan of San Mateo, California, that "you are right, however, about the need to show a new image. . . . We must rid ourselves of the 'country club-big business' image that we have (whether we deserve it or not). Then, of course, I believe we must use the '76 platform as a standard of principles and aggressively go out after the factory workers, the ethnic vote—which is some 40 million—and the shopkeepers and farmers. It isn't an easy job, but it must be done and done quickly if we are to save this land of ours. Anyway, I'm going to try. Thanks for your willingness to help."

A number of his correspondents after the 1976 elections were critical of Governor Reagan because they believed he refused to accept the vice-presidential nomination and because they thought he failed to campaign hard enough for President Ford. Neither charge was true, as the governor pointed out in rebuttal.

He wrote to Mr. and Mrs. Dick Crandall of Chico, California: "I don't know where the impression comes from that I abandoned ship in the general elections. You evidently have been misinformed.

"When the election got underway right after Labor Day I went out on the campaign trail, campaigning in twenty-five states for the entire ticket, including the president. My schedule was as heavy, or heavier, than it had been during the primary. In addition to my travels, at the president's request I did a series of TV commercials for national use. They ranged from 5 to 30 minutes each. I also did a 30-minute nationwide TV speech, which netted about $1,000,000. And, in addition, I sent out a letter over my signature which collected more than $1,000,000. The president and I appeared together at a closed circuit TV fund-raising dinner here in Los Angeles, which was the largest in the nation, and collected the most money.

"The day after the election, both Senator Dole and the president called me to thank me for what I had done, and the president said that in many of the states where he campaigned he found our people were manning the headquarters and doing the precinct walking. May I also point out that my campaign chairman became the co-chairman of the Ford campaign in California."

As a kind of an aside he also told the Crandalls: "While you didn't mention it—a few individuals have complained that had I been the vice-presidential candidate we might have won, and they also indicated that I turned this down. If that is your understanding, let me make it clear, I was *never asked* to be on the ticket." (The italicizing of "never asked" was his.)

In a letter to John A. Connors of Upper Saddle River, New Jersey, Governor Reagan went a little farther in talking about his campaigning for President Ford. "It is true that I might have done more. In fact, I pledged my cooperation to Mr. Ford on the night he won the nomination. But, despite a constant communication from our side, it was nearly a month later before the Ford Committee made specific requests for my help. By that time, of course, I was committed to helping many other Republican candidates. Despite this, I venture to say that I campaigned harder for

Mr. Ford than almost any other loser in a convention has ever campaigned for the victor.

"The fact is that Mr. Ford lost for a number of reasons, including his misstatement about Poland in the second debate. I do not believe that I am one of those reasons."

What Governor Reagan never pointed out in any of his letters is that neither he nor any of his chief political aides were invited to the general election campaign planning session President Ford and his people held in Vail, Colorado, immediately after the convention. This was in decided contrast to 1968 when one of the first things Republican candidate Richard Nixon did after the Republican convention was to invite Governor Reagan and his chief political aides to San Diego to confer on the role the governor might play in that year's campaign.

Governor Reagan made another reference to the vice presidency in a letter responding to W. B. Butcher of Tampa, Florida, who had written a particularly vitriolic letter. "You suggest that I could have had the vice presidential nomination on a Ford-Reagan ticket. President Ford had an opportunity to appoint a vice president when he assumed the office. He chose Nelson Rockefeller and never, at any time before, at, or after Kansas City mentioned me for the vice presidential spot."

Talk of the vice presidency always brings to mind Governor Reagan's choice for his own vice-presidential running mate, Senator Richard Schweiker of Pennsylvania.

The decision to pick a vice presidential running mate before the Republican National Convention and before the convention had picked its presidential nominee was a political one.

I am not aware if it was ever done before; certainly it had not been done in modern times.

The fact is, by July 1976, neither Governor Reagan nor President Ford had enough committed delegates to win the nomination, but President Ford was clearly ahead, and gaining. Something had to be done to reverse the momentum the Ford campaign was picking up.

John Sears, the Reagan campaign manager, had the idea of having Governor Reagan pick his vice presidential running mate in advance. He thought it would put the Ford campaign on the defensive and, with the right candidate, enable the Reagan campaign to pick up additional delegates.

Sears recommended to Governor Reagan that he pick Senator Schweiker. Schweiker had the reputation of being a liberal, but he was the senate seat mate of Senator Paul Laxalt, who was chairman of the Reagan campaign. Senator Laxalt had no trouble endorsing Senator Schweiker who, he said, was not all that liberal and really had much in common with the governor.

Sears felt that if Schweiker would accept the offer the Reagan campaign could pick up fifteen or twenty Pennsylvania delegates who were nominally uncommitted but who were under strong pressure to go with Ford.

Somewhat surprisingly, Senator Schweiker agreed to become Reagan's running mate if Reagan approved. He flew to California and spent a day meeting with Reagan, Laxalt, Sears, and a few other Reagan confidants and advisers.

The two men hit it off immediately, and Governor Reagan found that he and Senator Schweiker agreed on such issues as strong national defense, gun control, abortion, school prayer, and a number of other "social issues."

He also discovered that the senator had been coming gradually to the same conclusion that he, the governor, had reached many years earlier—that government and government spending are the source of all of our problems. In other words, Senator Schweiker was on the way to becoming a Reagan Republican well before the two decided to join forces.

But, of course, many people didn't know this. And the governor was the recipient of calls, letters, and even telegrams accusing him of betraying his principles and his supporters. Many old friends wanted to know "Why?"

In a letter to Robert Walker of Golden, Colorado, a former staffer and political aide, the governor wrote: "Contrary to what some have said, we are not that far apart in philosophy, and I don't think I compromised my principles. I found him in agreement with me on everything from amnesty to abortion and busing to gun control. We agree on

the death penalty, detente, inflation, and he has introduced
a constitutional amendment to restore prayer in the public
schools. He also believes we should be number one in
military strength."

He wrote the following letter to Mrs. Blanche Seaver of
Los Angeles, a long-time friend and political ally:

"Being on the road as I have been, there has been no
chance for a visit. I realize my surprise announcement must
have been a shock to you, but, I assure you, I have not
compromised my principles nor have I watered down my
conservatism one iota.

"I've been aware for some time of a division within our
party, both regional and, in a sense, philosophical. This
awareness has increased during the campaign. The Northeast Republicans are alienated from the rest of us, and much
of this is from lack of knowledge and understanding on
both sides. I firmly believe I was on the way to getting a
nomination but losing an election. The gap had to be
bridged.

"I didn't pull the senator out of a hat. His seat mate is
our chairman, Paul Laxalt, who, on the basis of their relationship, attests to his integrity and character. To look
only at a voting record based on a hand-picked selection
of votes is to ignore things far more indicative of his basic
philosophy. We found ourselves in agreement in our opposition to amnesty for draft-dodgers and deserters, abortion
on demand, forced busing, gun control, detente, and the
Helsinki pact. We support the death penalty and a stiffer
anti-crime program, as well as prayer in the schoolroom.
Senator Schweiker has introduced a constitutional amendment to restore prayer and Bible reading in public schools.
His record on national defense is sound, and he believes
we must once again become number one in military
strength.

"None of this would be true of such Republican liberals
as Rocky, Javits, Percy, Weicker, Case, etc. In other words,
Schweiker, in my view, is typical of the moderate Northeast
Republican, not the liberal fringe. He supported Goldwater
in 1964. Of course, we do have differences, but he will run

on the policies I've proposed and be pledged to those policies.

"We've all talked unity, but this is the first attempt anyone has ever made to do something about it, and it has been done by Conservatives holding out a hand without sacrificing our beliefs and principles. It is our effort to win an election, not a convention, and an election we *must* win if this land of ours is to remain free.

"I hope you'll give it a chance."

Since 1976, Senator Schweiker has constantly justified Governor Reagan's decision to pick him as his running mate. He opposed the Panama Canal treaties, introduced a welfare reform measure, and has a voting record that ranks among the most conservative in the senate.

The Cause Continues

SINCE 1976 POLITICS has never been far from Governor Reagan's mind.

Perhaps the most important political action he took after the election was to set up his own political action committee, Citizens for the Republic.

The organization's avowed purpose is to help elect conservative Republicans to office. Governor Reagan was its first chairman, and Senator Laxalt was chairman of its steering committee. Citizens for the Republic quickly became one of the best known and most successful of the conservative PACs. It supported more than a hundred candidates, put on political seminars, and published a semi-monthly newsletter. In addition, it picked up all of Governor Reagan's political expenses, thus allowing him to campaign for dozens of Republican candidates in the 1980 elections at no expense to them.

However, some people protested that he had set up CFTR for his own personal use. He wrote the following response to one of these persons, Mrs. Mary Davis of Valencia, California: "Now let me straighten you out, if I can, on our organization, the Citizens for the Republic which you charge is really for me alone. There were 800,000 dollars left over from my campaign.

"Under the new election laws, I could have kept that

money and used it for any purpose I saw fit, including a future campaign. However, by establishing the committee to work within the Republican Party to help elect congressmen, senators, state legislators, etc., I took a course that, should I ever become a candidate again, would limit a contribution from the committee to five thousand dollars. I think that should be evidence enough that I was trying to do something for the party and for what I believed in when I could have had the whole $800,000 for myself."

Mr. and Mrs. Robert P. Munger of Tucson, Arizona, thought he was trying to build a third party with the leftover campaign funds; funds that were left over, by the way, because they arrived too late to be spent. He explained to the Mungers that "I tried to figure what would be most in keeping with the desires of all of you who contributed the money. We are not starting a new party. Indeed I have rejected all proposals that a third party is the answer. My position is that the best way to build a new majority is to build it around the Republican Party.

"We are creating a committee called 'Citizens for the Republic' to work *within* the Republican Party and to help elect Republican congressmen. This will include developing candidates in districts we think are winnable.

"There will also be survey and research programs to provide Republican candidates with information that will be useful in their campaigns. I hope you will agree with this course of action."

CFTR originally was abbreviated to the initials CFR, but this brought protests from some who disliked the idea of its having the same initials as the Council on Foreign Relations, an organization which many conservatives are suspicious of.

He told R. W. Hanley of Prescott, Arizona, who called the CFR initials "the kiss of death," that "the T is there for the very thing you found objectionable. So did we."

Because he had come so close to unseating a sitting president of his own party, many persons thought Governor Reagan would be an ideal national chairman for the Republicans. He never gave serious thought to these proposals, however.

To Mrs. Donald D. Bendell of San Antonio, Texas, he wrote: "As to the national chairmanship, the fact that it is now a full-time salaried position, allowing for no outside activities (meaning I'd have to give up my five-day-a-week radio commentary which is on several hundred stations already and my syndicated newspaper column as well as much of my public speaking), rules that out.

"I truly believe I can do more outside the position than holding it."

He told Mr. and Mrs. Ed Vallen of Fontana, California, that "I believe we need a good tactician for this post, and I could be more effective by remaining a conservative spokesman through my newspaper column and radio broadcasts."

"Have no fear." he added, "I have every intention to remain active and do everything I can to rebuild the Republican party."

He was active indeed through the next three years, speaking out against the Panama Canal treaties, the breaking of relations with Taiwan, the administration's energy policies, and many other issues.

Panama undoubtedly was the issue that aroused the strongest feelings among voters. From the beginning Governor Reagan had said he was willing to talk to the Panamanians, but he was opposed to giving away the Panama Canal or the Canal Zone.

Here's what he wrote to Kathy Odom and Eric Pederson of Lake Wales, Florida:

"I will just send this to you, Kathy, but it is in answer to a letter from both of you.

"You asked for some reasons why I feel the way I do regarding the Panama Canal treaties. One reason can be found in a book by Lawrence Beilenson called, *The Treaty Trap*, which is probably the only book ever written about the history of the treaties. Going back over the thousands of years that men and governments have been writing such agreements, we find that invariably the treaties are broken the first time either nation finds it is to its advantage to do so. Add to that, we are dealing with a government that was not elected by the people; it seized power at the point of a gun, ejecting the duly elected president of Panama eleven days after he took office. This is the history of Panama. They have had more than fifty governments in their 60-plus years of existence. What assurances do we have that the present government will not treat us as he did the elected government of Panama, or that Torrijos won't be succeeded by a military overthrow. In the latter case we could face a government that—having now signed the treaty—would refuse to recognize it.

"Unfortunately, the answer to such a situation does not lie in our superior strength. International law today says that any nation can expropriate foreign owned property within its borders. If we ratify the treaties, we give up our right of sovereignty in the Canal Zone. This makes the Canal and our installations there only United States owned property. It could be expropriated the next day. Added to this, the United Nations charter says that no nation can resort to arms to redress such agreements; in other words, by our pledge to the U.N. we could not use our superior force to rectify a breaking of the treaty. This is exactly what Nasser, of Egypt, did to the British some 20-plus years ago, when he expropriated the British installations. When Britain threatened to use force, even the United States joined in telling Britain it could not do so.

"There is an additional factor, in spite of the vote by the Panamanians regarding the Canal. Under the present dictatorship there is no way of knowing if it reflected the true feeling of the people of Panama. By making this deal we would be strengthening the hold the dictator has over his people and according to Freedom House, the liberal, nonprofit organization which monitors freedom all over the world, Panama ranks alongside the Soviet Union and Cuba as a violator of human rights.

"We of the United States have nothing to be ashamed of in the Canal's history. There would be no Panama had it not been for the Canal. No other nation could have built it; we made Panama a nation with a death rate lower than our own due to our conquering of yellow fever. We have run the Canal at no profit, never recovered the original cost, and have made Panama the nation with the highest standard of living in Central America. The Canal is responsible for one-fourth of Panama's gross national product, and that fairly well sums up why I feel as I do."

He met with Sol M. Linowitz, President Carter's negotiator of the treaties and later exchanged correspondence with him. In one letter, he told Linowitz: "I must say, however, that I still believe we are on the wrong path. That's not to say that we shouldn't negotiate if there are friction points we can eliminate, but that the negotiations should not be based on giving up our rights of sovereignty in the Zone.

"Since our meeting, I've had an opportunity to talk with people from some other Latin American countries. Contrary to the idea that we would gather new friends by giving up the Canal, they expressed very bluntly their opinion of what is going on. They asked why the United States doesn't just say no and then made it plain they would think more highly of us if we did. I tend to agree. I recognize, of course, that it's not a simple problem. But, I must confess, I remain firmly convinced that our country should not, at this time, give the appearance of backing down on this particular issue."

To Panamanian citizen Arthur McGowan, Reagan wrote:
"I'm sorry you feel as you do and assure you that I have not only studied the treaties, but have had the best of legal advice.

"You proceed from the viewpoint that the treaties will be observed to the letter, and I can understand your doing so. I, on the other hand, take into consideration the fact that back through history *no* treaty has ever been observed if it suited a nation's interest to break it. This, I might add, is true of my country as well.

"Perhaps the problem that makes this particular situation so difficult is that we are dealing with a transfer of property (highly strategic property in a very dangerous world), not just a pledge of mutual support or the other things usually resolved by treaties. If this treaty is violated, the results are immediate and catastrophic.

"Further complicating the situation are matters of international law and the United Nations charter which you have ignored in your letter. International law now says a nation can expropriate foreign-owned property within its borders. The United Nations charter says no nation can use force to prevent expropriation. Once the treaties are ratified, our canal facilities are foreign-owned property within Panama's borders. The Suez Canal is a perfect example of what I'm talking about.

"There is enough ambiguity in the treaty language that even now your government and mine are in disagreement as to certain aspects of their meaning. What happens when new people, not party to these negotiations, years hence find different interpretations of their own?

"Arturo, as I said to you, I believe there are things we could negotiate between our two countries that would eliminate friction and benefit Panama economically and in other ways. I will support such negotiations, but I cannot believe in these treaties. I'm sorry you feel as you do because I have to carry on this fight. However, I had hoped we had begun a friendship which could continue in spite of our disagreement."

Governor Reagan made three additional points in a letter to Manfred Rosenow of Bogota, Colombia:

1. If the Canal is no longer sufficiently important to the United States to keep it (as some of its advocates suggest), then why don't we just give it away without paying some $80 a year to have it taken off our hands?

2. Why do we, in the treaties, give up the right to build another Canal (that would not be obsolete) in another country? If the present Canal is obsolete and we feel we need a better Canal, why not make a deal with another country?

3. Finally, there is a fatal flaw in these treaties, in that by giving up our rights of sovereignty in the Zone, the Canal installations become simply foreign-owned property within the borders of Panama. We thus relinquish the firm basis that undergirds our presence there and ensures our ability to guarantee the Canal's security. International law now dictates that

any nation can expropriate foreign-owned property, and the United Nations charter says that no nation, whose property has been seized, can resort to armed force to redress any grievance. In other words, if we relinquish our present right—as the treaty would do—Panama could expropriate the Canal any time after they went into effect, and we could not even use the forces stationed there to resist. Remember the case of the Suez Canal, when Nasser, in violation of his treaty, seized the British installations. When they threatened the use of force, even the United States joined the Soviet Union and others in forcing them to back away and let Nasser keep the Canal.

In a letter to Denison Kitchel of Phoenix, Barry Goldwater's 1964 campaign chairman, the governor explained how the Panama Canal became an issue:

"First of all, I did not set out to make this an issue in last year's campaign. In fact, while I knew the negotiations were going on, I was confident they wouldn't get anywhere, since thirty-eight senators had signed the pledge not to ratify the treaty. It never entered my mind to even mention the Canal.

"But, as you know, in New Hampshire you don't make speeches, you go to town hall meetings and answer questions. I'll never forget the first meeting, and the question from the floor about the Canal. The audience looked at the questioner as if he'd announced the end of the world, then back at me as if to say, what's he talking about? I told them about the negotiations and gave my own opinion as to what we should do. This experience was repeated time after time, both there and in Florida, until it did become an issue, made so by the people. Then in Texas, Jerry made the great mistake of trying to deny it, and the feathers hit the fan."

Sadly, the Canal issue came close to bringing about a rift between two old friends, Governor Reagan and the late John Wayne. Wayne favored the treaties, and neither was able to convince the other of the rightness of his views. In one letter to Wayne the governor explained that he had just returned from a speaking trip and found a letter from

Wayne. "I'm glad you closed it with a declaration of your continuing friendship for Nancy and myself. I'm sure you must know the deep affection we have for you and that our disagreement over these treaties will not affect or lessen that affection."

He closed the letter this way: "Duke, I hope and pray that as this issue heats up and we seem to be destined to be on opposite sides that we can keep it from affecting a friendship both Nancy and I treasure."

Potpourri

THIS CHAPTER IS a potpourri of some of Reagan's letters written mostly to young people since the 1976 Republican National Convention. They reflect his continuing faith in God and in America and its people.

Early in 1978 Richard McCann of Lubbock, Texas, wrote asking him what it means to be an American. Governor Reagan responded:

"I wish I had some neat paragraph to sum it up. I happen to believe right now that we are temporarily off the track in a number of ways, but I am an optimist and a believer in the American people enough to think this is only a temporary phase and that the basic strength of America still remains.

"To be an American means that we have descended from people of virtually every ethnic and racial background who must have had some extra love of freedom and courage to uproot themselves and come to a strange land. Whether they be the most recent immigrants or our forefathers from several generations back, they brought with them the prejudices of their native lands. But here, living in this melting pot, they gradually found that in talking to each other instead of about each other, they could live and work together.

"To be an American means living in a land where for the first time in man's history, the genius of the individual

211

was freed, released to carry him as high and as far as his own ability and talents and effort could take him.

"To be an American is to live under a system in which those who govern do so limited in power to that which the people themselves grant them. The government can have no power which has not first been granted to it by the people, and the people can grant to government no power they themselves as individuals don't possess.

"To be an American is to be something of a new breed made up of that mix from all over the world with a distinct personality that caused Winston Churchill to say of us, 'We seem to be the only men who can laugh and fight at the same time.'

"We have a generosity that makes us voluntarily support more good causes and worthwhile undertakings than all the rest of the world put together. It caused Pope Piux XII at the end of World War II, when American power was all that stood between the world and the dark ages, to say the American people have a genius for great and unselfish deeds.

"Into the hands of America God has placed an afflicted mankind. Our belief in the individual and his sanctity is so great that our philosophy is that we will collectively go to the aid of even the least among us wherever he may be in the world if his God-given rights are being unjustly denied him.

"I truly believe that to be an American is to be a part of a nation with a destiny that God put this land here between the great oceans to be discovered by a special kind of people and that God intended America to be free."

Nicole Bosco, a student from Agoura, California, wrote that she was doing a paper on him. She asked for his views on several issues, including women's rights. The governor replied in part:

"I support equal rights for all people and believe there are still some areas of discrimination where women are concerned that could stand correcting. I'm concerned though about the Equal Rights Amendment. I fear this simple sounding proposal could wind up taking more from women than they would gain. Where there is something that needs correcting, let's correct it by a specific law not a constitutional amendment.

"Racial discrimination? We've come a very long way in the right direction since I was a boy in Dixon, Illinois. I like to think my generation had something to do with that because we were the first to recognize there was a racial problem and started doing something about it.

"When I broadcasted baseball, no blacks were allowed to play. I used to editorialize against this. So did many others, and one day we broke through and eliminated this terribly unfair discrimination. Prejudice and bigotry are things we must all fight against. They are based on ignorance and are one of mankind's greatest stupidities.

"That brings me to busing and here this may seem strange, but I'm against it. It has increased the very bitterness we're trying to cure. California State Superintendent of Education Wilson Riles—himself a black—is opposed to it and said it better than anyone: 'It is degrading and insulting to tell a black child he or she can only learn if they are sitting between two white children.'

"On foreign aid, I believe we've gotten off the track. We are told if you give a hungry man a fish, he'll be hungry again tomorrow. If you teach him how to fish, he'll never be hungry again. Our foreign aid hasn't made the people we want to help self-sufficient. Let's really help by teaching them how to provide for themselves.

"My political philosophy has been called conservative. I don't know if that is the proper word or not. I believe our system was created to give the ultimate in individual freedom consistent with an orderly society. Government exists to protect us from each other—not from ourselves. I think government has gotten too big, too costly, and is robbing us of liberty. I'd like to see many things now done in Washington, done at the state and local level where government is closer to the people."

Governor Reagan's files identify the recipient of the following letter only as "Michael." The letter is short but it is advice that young Michael probably will never forget.

"Dear Michael:

"I'm proud to be a part of your scrapbook. Naturally,

I'm tempted to offer advice, so here goes. Let your scrap-book be a reminder that what man can dream, man can do. Whether your dreams of what you'll be may change with the years, believe always that God has a plan for each one of us.

"Thomas Wolfe said it all—'The right of every man to be what God intended him to be. That is the dream of America.'

Best Regards,
Ronald Reagan"

Ronald Reagan is constantly upbeat about our country. Those who say that he does nothing but criticize speak from preconceived notions. Typical of his positive approach is this letter to the students of the fifth grade at the Thirty-Second Street School in Los Angeles.

"My thanks to all of you for sending me the paper you wrote called, 'America My Country.' But, even more, thank you for writing that paper. It means a great deal to me that you would want me to have it, but I must also tell you how moved I was by the beauty of the things you had to say about this land of ours.

"As the years go on, you will meet many people who will try to tell you so many things that are wrong with America—people who are unhappy about one thing or another and who think this country has let them down some-how. Keep your faith and remember these things you have written. This country will *never* let us down. There are, sometimes, people who let the country down, but I don't think that will include any of you.

"In the year 1630, a tiny sailing ship, the *Arabella*, lay at anchor off the snow-covered coast of Massachusetts. On board John Winthrop gathered those first pilgrims together and spoke to them. He said, 'We shall be as a city upon a hill and the eyes of all mankind will be upon us.'

"After reading your fine paper, I am more than ever certain that we shall, indeed, be that shining city upon a hill."

But, though an optimist, Governor Reagan is no Pol-lyana; he does not wear rose-colored glasses. He sees clearly the dangers to our country that too much government, too powerful a bureaucracy can bring.

He wrote the following, lengthy letter regarding such dangers and giving specific examples, to Walter Langhorst and the Second Period Social Studies 11H Class of Kings Park, New York, Senior High School.

"Some of the members of your class have asked me to write my views on conservatism, or conservative policy, so called. I am delighted to do this and, Mr. Langhorst, I want to commend you for seeing that the members of your class get all sides to the questions of the day and are exposed to more than one viewpoint.

"When I said conservative policy, so called, I put it that way because I feel very deeply that the words 'liberal' and 'conservative' have somehow become reversed and that they no longer have the classical meaning of the words. Two hundred years ago today's conservatives, I believe, would have been the liberals who were fighting against the power of the throne. They would have been classed among the Tories, who wanted to continue the authority of the central government in England. I say this because today the so-called 'liberal' movement is one dedicated to seeking government solutions at the federal level for most of the problems besetting us. The conservative, on the other hand, is a believer in reducing the power and size of the federal government and returning authority and autonomy to the states and the local communities to those levels of government closer to the people.

"Let me use education itself as an example. In this country at the local school district level we built one of the greatest public school systems in all the world. In recent years a thing called federal aid to education came into existence. Now, the conservative view is that if the federal government had simply made tax resources, which it had preempted, available at the local level, there would have been no need for federal aid. And, of course, with federal aid has come federal control.

"The federal government's excuse for getting into the act was, they said, that local governments no longer had the resources. A group of distinguished educators went to

Washington when this subject was under discussion and made a proposal that would have provided the funding. The director of education at that time, Francis Keppel, said, 'You don't understand that under such a plan we couldn't realize our social objectives.'

"As the federal bureaucracy has grown those social objectives are becoming more clear. We are governed by regulations—tens of thousands of them—not laws; regulations that are dictated by permanent employees of government, not our elected representatives. Under those regulations, for example, in Connecticut a sixth grade boys' choir, long a tradition in the community, was forced to disband because it violated the HEW guidelines against sex discrimination. They say that musical groups can only be divided now on a basis of vocal range; but in the sixth grade the boys still sing soprano!

"At the University of Washington in Seattle the Association of Faculty Wives has been ordered to disband unless it will admit men.

"The National Education Association, headquartered in Washington, D.C., has made it plain that it believes in a federal school system. I believe that in a country as diverse as the United States, we will be far better off with our traditional system governed by local school boards where parents, teachers, and the people of the community can have a say as to the education their sons and daughters will receive.

"Let me talk for a moment on the growth of government. When I sat where you are now sitting, the governments of the United States—federal, state, and local together—only took a dime from every dollar earned, and less than a third of that paid for the whole federal government. Today, those governments are taking forty-four cents out of every dollar earned, and two-thirds of that goes to Washington.

"Now a gigantic increase in social security tax has been passed. This is probably one of the biggest tax increases ever made at one time in the history of the world. First of all, not too many years ago social security didn't call it a tax; they said it was an insurance program and one day we would get our own money back plus the interest paid on it. When you go into the work force you will find that the social security tax you will pay into government will be more than twice as much as you can ever hope to receive back from social security. The governing board of social security recently admitted that the program is, and brace yourselves, $17 trillion out of balance. Now that is in constant dollars; if we allow for inflation and that inflation might continue on as it has for these past couple of years then that $17 trillion figure could be as much as 250 trillion dollars.

"These are, of course, simply horror stories about what happens when government assumes too much power and attempts to do things that are not the government's proper province.

"I would like to tell you also about the free enterprise system versus the liberal position of government control and regulation of business and industry. The president of the Eli Lilly Pharmaceutical Company, one of our major pharmaceutical firms, has stated that his company now spends more man hours per year filling out government-required paper work than in the research of cancer and heart disease combined. This regulation of the drug business has added fifty cents to the cost of every prescription written.

"This is true of other businesses too. There is a belief in the federal establishment that business and industry can no longer engage in the free marketplace without all those government regulations. Economists have pointed out that if unnecessary regulation of business could be eliminated, it would reduce the present inflation rate by half.

"Let me give you an example. Let's take an island, Manhattan Island, millions of people, millions of businesses of every kind. You can walk down the streets of New York and decide whether to eat Italian food in an Italian restaurant or go to a German or Chinese restaurant, a French cafe, well, you name it. All of these are private businesses and, of course, there are little shops located sometimes in spaces not more than eight feet wide between some of the great skyscrapers. They have their own clientele, customers who come to them for various things from neckties to shirts, haberdashery to pharmacy, where people go in for razor-blades, hairpins, and whatnot.

"Now, every day thousands and thousands of trucks, trains, boats, and airplanes come to that island to unload the millions of items that are the result of millions of independent decisions—the little shopkeeper ordering "x" number of pocket combs, the restaurants ordering the varieties of food, etc. If one of those shopkeepers orders too much of a certain kind of toothpaste for his business, he has made a mistake and he rectifies it by having a sale, cutting the price to at least get back his investment. If he hasn't bought enough and a customer comes in and asks to buy what he can't provide, the customer has a choice; he can either take another brand or he can walk down the street to another shop and get what he wants.

"Try to envision the size bureau it would take if the government had to make all those millions of decisions, to dictate how many combs and what kind, how many tubes of toothpaste, what kinds of food, etc., and what would come into Manhattan. Our free marketplace runs very well based on the decisions all of those people are making in their own best interest, meaning that they buy what they guess their customers want. Then we, the customers, register a vote for or against competing articles.

"The only way the government could substitute for those independent decisions would be to do it the way they do it in the Soviet Union. You wouldn't have a choice. Every restaurant would have the same kind of menu, and this is true in the Russian restaurants. There would only be one kind of toothpaste; the one the government dictated. In other words, it would be a little bit like everyone in the Army getting his G.I. issue of clothing, supplies, etc.

"The conservative position is to have faith in the marketplace. The energy situation is a perfect example of the two positions. The liberal philosophy prevalent today in Washington is that the government must have a program to solve the energy shortage, but the government caused the energy shortage by price controls and regulations they began imposing on the oil and gas industry back in the 1950's. We are now importing more oil from the Arab states than during the time of the embargo. We are producing less here in our own country, and government, instead of getting out of the way and letting the incentives of the marketplace encourage people to go out and drill and/or find new sources of energy, tells us all to drive 55 miles per hour, set the thermostats down, and save what we have. Government offers no inducement except to put a higher tax on fuel which will go to the government, not to someone who might be encouraged to drill a well. And they can't understand why the problem isn't solved!

"The new energy agency in Washington has 20,000 employees and a $10.5 billion budget to start with. That amounts to 10¢ a gallon on every gallon of gasoline we are going to buy in the coming year. Yet there is nothing in the government-proposed program to encourage finding more sources of energy.

"Back in the middle 1800's we had an energy shortage. Most of the houses in America were lighted with whale oil. When the whales became scarce the price of whale oil skyrocketed. Government didn't do a thing, they didn't lift a finger, but all over things began to happen. In Pennsylvania someone thought possibly the sticky stuff coming out of the ground here and there could be used. The result was Pennsylvania oil, and the discovery and manufacture of kerosene which could be made, produced, and sold for a few cents a gallon. Suddenly there was no energy shortage, and the homes were lighted, probably better than they had been with whale oil. Government hadn't done a thing to help. It had been done by people who saw the price of whale oil go up and knew there would be a market for anyone who could find a way to provide light for the people's homes. That is the free market. That is private enterprise.

"I realize this is getting very long, so maybe I just better close. If you want to ask me any questions, I will write another letter, but let me add this one thing. In a totally government-managed program like the Soviet Union, you would be told what your education would result in, you would be told what line of work you were going to do when you got out of school or whether or not you could go on to college. Here you are free to make your own choice; to try to succeed if you can or fail if you want to.

"A very good measuring stick for a government program is this—Isn't it government's function to protect us from each other, not to try and protect us from ourselves?

"I hope this has been of some help with regard to my views on conservatism, and as I say, if you have any questions you would like to ask just give me the word, and I'll write some more.

"Thanks for the opportunity, and best of luck."

The governor wrote a shorter letter to Mrs. Whitehead's Social Studies Class at Valhall High School, El Cajon, California. The letter was in response to a note from Dr. Charles G. Eller telling him that "my daughter is a ninth-grade student in a high school in a predominately Republican area. Enclosed is a copy of their work sheet in Social Science class. To me, the 'Liberal' and 'Conservative' definitions make the Republicans look like the 'bad' guys. I resent my tax dollars being spent in this matter.

"Would you be kind enough to take a moment to clarify for the class your definition of a conservative? I would appreciate it, and perhaps our young teachers might even learn something."

Governor Reagan's letter to the class said:

"A short time ago, I was shown a work sheet for your class, defining and comparing some of the labels commonly used in political dialogue and giving examples of each.

"I couldn't help but write, hoping you'll forgive my being so presumptuous. You see, I saw a comparison similar to your work sheet on a blackboard in another high school just a few years ago.

"For most of my adult life, I was a New Deal Democrat and considered to be a liberal. Now I am Republican and called a conservative. However, I happen to believe that the labels 'liberal' and 'conservative' are misleading terms. In the work sheet, liberals were identified as having faith in the common man and, conversely, conservatives as lacking in that faith. Democrats were given as an example of liberalism and Republicans as one of conservatism.

"It is precisely because the opposite is true that I changed parties. For some decades now, the liberal movement has worked to centralize government authority in Washington and to increase government's power. They justify this on the ground that the world has grown so complex that we can no longer afford as much individual freedom as we had when I was in high school.

"They theorize that an elite in the nation's capital is better qualified than we as individuals are to determine our own destiny. Thus, they have, over the last four decades, given powers once vested in the states, local communities, and school districts to the federal government. Example— the Wethersfield, Connecticut, sixth grade boys' choir has been disbanded on orders from H.E.W. in Washington because it violates sex discrimination guidelines laid down by H.E.W. At the University of Seattle, the 'Faculty Wives Association' has been ordered to disband unless it takes in men. Of course, men are husbands, not wives.

"Today's conservative believes the federal government is too big and too powerful; that authority for many government programs should be returned to the states and local governments, and that no one knows what is good for the people (the common man) so well as the people themselves.

"We find the ultimate in government planning in the Soviet Union. There, on a high school graduation day, a government representative reads off the graduates' names and tells each one where he or she will report to work and what kind of work they'll do. Others are told they will go on to further education. I think you believe you are best able to decide what your life's work will be.

"Actually, libertarianism is at the very heart of conservatism; the God-given right of each one of you to determine your own destiny and to have the ultimate in individual freedom consistent with an orderly society. That's why— believing in that—I'm a conservative."

Belinda Long of Pierceton, Indiana, asked about the family side of politics and if he was able to spend enough time with his family. He wrote back:

"I suppose I could answer the first one by saying that none of us, in any line of work, gets to spend as much time with our families as we would like to. Politics can make it even more difficult, but Nancy and I made up our minds, when I became governor, that we were not going to use public office as an excuse, and we set out deliberately and worked very hard to keep life at home as normal as it had always been, and it can be done.

"I was surprised to learn how busy public life can be. Like everyone else, I thought of politicians as not working very hard and having a lot of frills with the job, such as banquets and dinners, etc. I found that it wasn't true, and that the job is totally consuming. I don't know of anything I have done in my life that had longer hours, more continuously, than the office I held. I also must say, however, it was the most personally fulfilling experience of my entire life. There were some nights when I would go home feeling ten feet tall, because of something I had been able to do that I thought would benefit the people.

"I think all of us should take an interest in public life. Government by the people means participating, keeping abreast of what's going on, being aware of what our elected representatives are doing, and making our wishes known to those representatives. This takes some time, but the alternative to running politics by the people, is letting people be run by politicians."

One letter Governor Reagan wrote was primarily an article for the *Dingy*, the school newspaper of Bellport Senior High School, Brookhaven, New York. The inspirational story again reflects his feeling for our country.

"Not long ago, we learned that the Soviet Union had just awarded its highest honor, the Soviet Gold Medal, to the man who murdered Leon Trotsky. Trotsky, Stalin's enemy, was in exile in Mexico. The killer had served twenty years in a Mexican prison after sinking an ice axe into his victim's skull.

"My memory went back to an American who won our highest award, the Congressional Medal of Honor, in World War II. The contrast between what the two nations saw as worthy of such recognition tells us a great deal about our relative values. A B-17 bomber, returning from a raid over Germany, had been badly shot up. The ball turret beneath the belly of the plane had been hit and the gunner wounded. The turret was jammed so he couldn't be removed.

"The plane was losing altitude and, finally, over the channel, the captain gave the order to bail out. As the kid in the ball turret saw the other crew members start to jump, he cried out in terror, realizing he was being left to go down with the plane. The last man to leave saw the captain sit down on the floor of the plane. He took the boy's hand and said, 'Never mind son, we'll ride it down together.' The Congressional Medal of Honor was posthumously awarded.

"One country awards murder; ours recognized the nobility of a sacrifice made to bring comfort and human companionship to a young man in the last few moments of his life."

To Mrs. Carole Anne Slobin of Fullerton, California, Governor Reagan wrote in 1977:

"I've always believed we should pay our way for the good things life has given us so I have worked for candidates and causes I believed in since the end of World War II when I was in my early 30's. I never believed I would ever seek public office myself and must say I did resist when a group tried to persuade me to run for governor in 1966. They persuaded me to become a reluctant candidate. Let me add, however, that those eight years as governor were the most fulfilling of my entire life.

"I think the two things I'm most proud of in those years were, first, the restoration of solvency to the state; getting it out of debt and then returning to the taxpayers some 5.7 billion in tax rebates and, second, the welfare reforms which reduced the rolls by some 400,000 people who were not really eligible for help. We saved the taxpayers $2 billion in three years and also raised the grants to the deserving needy by 43 percent.

"I want to see our country return to fiscal sanity and stop spending more than we take in. This will end inflation and solve our unemployment problem. We should eliminate the unwarranted regulations by government which touch every facet of our lives and the excessive and useless paperwork the government requires of individuals and businesses. On the world scene, I would like to see us accept our leadership of the free world and conduct foreign affairs on the basis, not of expediency, but of what is morally the right thing to do.

"I would hope we can recognize the realism of the threat to world freedom the Soviet Union represents. With that realization, we should have the will to restore our capability to make foreign aggressors unwilling to test our strength. If we do this, your pupils will be able to grow up in peace and with the assurance of continued freedom. And that brings me to what my hopes are for young Americans.

"First of all, I hope they can once again know the freedom I had when I was their age. And I hope they will understand how much there is to love in this way of life and this land we call America."

Finally, to Kevin G. Smith of San Jose, California, he wrote:

"The revolution 200 years ago was unlike any other revolution in history. It didn't simply replace one set of rulers with another. It was a philosophical revolution.

"For the first time since man first began his long climb from the swamp to the stars the genius of each individual was freed to perform such miracles of invention, construction, and production as the world had never seen. In these 200 years since that revolution half the economic activity in the entire history of mankind has taken place in these United States of America.

"One has to conclude that the single catalyst bringing this about was individual freedom; this concept that government's only power is that granted to it voluntarily by the people; that man is free by reason of birth alone and has the God-given dignity of determining his own destiny.

"There are those among us and abroad in the world who preach a doctrine they claim is new and revolutionary, but which is in truth merely a return to the days of feudalism wherein man is the servant of the state. If we are to fulfill our destiny we must repudiate them as false prophets, for we are the last best hope of man on earth."

Revealing, Intimate, Fascinating—True-Life Portraits of the Great and the Powerful

__**A TIME TO HEAL**   04693-1—$2.95
Gerald R. Ford

__**THE LONELY**   04253-7—$2.50
LADY OF SAN CLEMENTE
Lester David

__**ON EAGLES'**   04022-4—$2.50
WINGS
Ezer Weizman

__**PLAIN SPEAKING—** 03746-0—$2.50
AN ORAL BIOGRAPHY OF
HARRY S. TRUMAN
Merle Miller

__**REFLECTIONS**   04637-0—$2.95
WITHOUT MIRRORS
Louis Nizer

__**ROBERT F.**   04047-X—$2.50
KENNEDY: A MEMOIR
Jack Newfield

__**THE SEARCH**   03354-6—$2.25
FOR JFK
Joan and Clay Blair, Jr.

Berkley Book Mailing Service
P.O. Box 690
Rockville Centre, NY 11570

Please send me the above titles. I am enclosing $
(Please add 50¢ per copy to cover postage and handling). Send check or
money order—no cash or C.O.D.'s. Allow six weeks for delivery.

NAME

ADDRESS

CITY   STATE/ZIP   61J

Bestsellers from Berkley
The books you've been hearing about—and want to read

__	**HIGH GLOSS** Peter Engel	04542-0—$2.50
__	**ABINGDON'S** Michael French	04479-3—$2.50
__	**THE THIRD WORLD WAR:** **AUGUST 1985** General Sir John Hackett, et al.	04477-7—$2.95
__	**SELF-PORTRAIT** Gene Tierney, with Mickey Herskowitz	04485-8—$2.75
__	**THE WINNER'S CIRCLE** Charles Paul Conn	04500-5—$2.50
__	**MOMMIE DEAREST** Christina Crawford	04444-0—$2.75
__	**NURSE** Peggy Anderson	04685-0—$2.75
__	**THE SIXTH COMMANDMENT** Lawrence Sanders	04271-5—$2.75
__	**MANHATTAN** Neal Travis	04294-4—$2.50
__	**THE HEALERS** Gerald Green	04451-3—$2.75

Berkley Book Mailing Service
P.O. Box 690
Rockville Centre, NY 11570

Please send me the above titles. I am enclosing $ ____
(Please add 50¢ per copy to cover postage and handling). Send check or
money order—no cash or C.O.D.'s. Allow six weeks for delivery.

NAME

ADDRESS

CITY   STATE/ZIP

1J